Transforming the Stone

Transforming the Stone

Preaching Through Resistance to Change

Barbara K. Lundblad

Abingdon Press
Nashville

TRANSFORMING THE STONE:
PREACHING THROUGH RESISTANCE TO CHANGE

This book is printed on recycled, acid-free paper.

Library of Congress Cataloging-in-Publication Data

Lundblad, Barbara K., 1944-
Transforming the stone : preaching through resistance to change / Barbara K. Lundblad.
p. cm.
Includes bibliographical references (p.).
ISBN 0-687-09613-8 (alk. paper)
1. Church renewal—Sermons. I. Title.

BV600.2 .L85 2001
251—dc21

2001022492

01 02 03 04 05 06 07 08 09 10—10 9 8 7 6 5 4 3 2 1

MANUFACTURED IN THE UNITED STATES OF AMERICA

In memory of my father

Harold Hemborg Lundblad

1918 – 1996

And in continuing gratitude for my mother

Ilene Bloomquist Lundblad

Contents

Acknowledgments

Over the past months I have thought so much about stones that I see them everywhere. I have remembered stones I had long forgotten: the rock pile on our farm where my sister and I went "mining," armed with hammers to break off pieces of "gold" glistening in the sun; the flat rock ledges in the boundary waters canoe area where I joined my youth group gazing up at the northern lights; the Manhattan schist that rose up behind our church building in New York, creating a sense of wilderness in the midst of the city; the huge boulders along the Maine coast that look as though they had been dropped there by the hand of God.

So it is that this book has emerged from memories—from years on the farm, from two decades in the city and in the parish. This book wasn't created *ex nihilo* but took shape from what was already there. It seems a bit like Michelangelo's "Captives" struggling out of the solid slabs that held them—an arm, a torso, a face emerging from the stone into the light of day. The sculptor had the sense that these figures were there all the time, waiting to be discovered.

I am deeply grateful to the members of Our Saviour's Atonement Lutheran Church in New York City, who taught me most of what I know about preaching. Their lively engagement with lectionary texts over shared meals and their honest responses to seventeen years of sermons transformed the way I understand preaching and listening. Most of the sermons in this book began in that parish and were later reshaped for *The Protestant Hour* radio program; thus, the sermons have lost some of the specificity of a particular setting in order to reach radio listeners I never met. I will always be grateful to those listeners who wrote to me sharing their insights as well as their disagreements.

Since joining the faculty of Union Theological Seminary in New York City, I have learned much from my students, people of many different denominations and myriad life experiences. Their lively intellects and passion for social transformation continue to challenge me every time we gather for class. The last sermon in this book was preached at daily worship in Union's James Chapel. I am deeply indebted to my colleagues in the Arts and Ministry Field: Mary Boys, Ana Maria Diaz-Stevens, Kathleen Talvacchia, Ann Belford Ulanov and Janet Walton. They read stacks of sermons and encouraged this project all along the way. Robert Seaver, my teaching partner, has graced me with the wisdom of over fifty years of teaching at Union. When Bob reads the Bible I almost always say, "I have never heard that text before!" though I have heard it a hundred times.

I remain humbly grateful for God's call to preach the good news that has power to transform the lives of individuals and communities. Perhaps I have learned the most from those who are terrified of change. I pray that together we will continue to be open to the Spirit's tutoring even in the midst of our fear.

Barbara K. Lundblad
Lent 2001

Introduction

Transformation is a word far bigger than this page. The word speaks change—change so deep that nothing will ever be the same. Such change encompasses what happens in the life of one individual as well as what happens within whole communities and nations. We use various forms of the word in everyday speech: "She was transformed by her experience of living with the poor in Guatemala," or "The global economy has completely transformed the role of governments and nation-states." The change might be positive or negative: Will the transformation caused by the Internet build or break down a sense of community? What will the transformation of American agriculture by huge corporations mean for rural communities and congregations?

In the New Testament, *transformation* sometimes comes from the Greek word *metamorphoo*. When we were in grade school, many of us learned the long word *metamorphosis* to describe what happened when a butterfly emerged from its cocoon and stretched its wings. We could hardly believe our eyes, for the beautiful winged creature bore no resemblance to the empty shell it left behind. Anyone who has been invited to hear a friend's story at an open AA meeting has heard and seen an equally dramatic metamorphosis. When the story ends we stammer our disbelief: "I can't believe you're the person you were talking about!"

The New Testament, however, uses *metamorphoo* sparingly. In Matthew 17 and Mark 9 the Greek is translated as "transfigured" to describe the profound change in Jesus' appearance on the mountain. The dazzling sight caused not only awe, but fear in the disciples. In 2 Corinthians, *metamorphoo* is translated as "transformed," portraying the profound change that happens in the lives of believers: "And all of us, with unveiled faces, seeing the glory of the Lord as though reflected in a mirror, are *being transformed* into the same image from one degree of glory to another; for this comes from the Lord, the Spirit" (2 Cor. 3:18; emphasis added).

For the apostle Paul, such internal transformation reshaped all of life for both individuals and community: "Do not be conformed to this world, but *be transformed* by the renewing of your minds, so that you may discern what is the will of God—what is good and acceptable and perfect" (Rom. 12:2; emphasis added). Paul isn't speaking primarily of individual transformation, but rather of "your minds"—plural. In this chapter he goes on to say that such transformation reshapes separate individuals into nothing less than the corporate Body of Christ.

But scripture is not limited to *metamorphoo* when speaking of transformation. Sometimes transformation completely reshapes an individual life, which is often marked by a change of name. Mary sang not only of changes in her own life, but of seismic shifts in the whole social order: the mighty brought low and the lowly lifted up. The writer of 1 Peter uses a pair of opposites to portray the transformation of a people: "Once you were not a people, but now you are God's people; once you had not received mercy, but now you have received mercy" (2:10). Transformation is not limited to human beings; Isaiah prophesied that the land itself would be transformed. "The wilderness and the dry land shall be glad, the desert shall rejoice and blossom; like the crocus, it shall blossom abundantly, and rejoice with joy and singing" (Isa. 35:1-2*a*). And in the fullness of time all creation will be transformed. There will be "a new heaven and a new earth"; the water of life will flow from God's throne, and the leaves of the tree of life growing on its banks will be for the "healing of the nations" (Rev. 21:1; 22:1-2).

Teaching Transformation as a Gift

For people of faith, transformation doesn't *happen*: it is a gift from God. Even as the Spirit of God hovered over the deep bringing forth creation, so now the Spirit revivifies all of life. Transformation is God's doing. Ever since the day God formed us from the dust of earth and "inspirited" us to life, human beings have been called into partnership with the Creator. We may indeed pray, "O God, transform this world of pain," but God seldom works alone. In the Small Catechism, Martin Luther asks the meaning of the second petition of the Lord's Prayer: "What does ['Thy kingdom come'] mean?" Then he answers his question: "To be sure, the kingdom of God comes of itself, without our prayer, but we pray in this petition that it may also come to us."[1]

Likewise, we pray that God's gift of *transformation* "may also come to us." We pray that this word that is too big for any page will be enfleshed in our midst. Those of us called to preach pray that our sermons will be vehicles for Spirit-borne change in the lives of individuals and congregations. We pray that our congregations and church bodies will bear this word of transformation within the larger world.

In *Cadences of Home: Preaching among Exiles,* Walter Brueggemann describes the process of transformation:

> We now know (or think we know) that human transformation (the way people change) does not happen through didacticism or through excessive certitude, but through the playful entertainment of another scripting of reality that may subvert the old given text and its interpretation and lead to the embrace of an alternative text and its redescription of reality.[2]

Brueggemann's words hold seeds of promise, but also hints of danger. Subverting the old given text may be very threatening. Some will surely want to hold on to the old script. The "alternative text and its redescription of reality" will not be eagerly embraced by everyone. While some will be filled with joy, others will be shaken and afraid.

Preaching Transformation in the Midst of Fear

"The Nurturing Place" in Jersey City welcomes and nurtures children whose families are homeless. Few people would have heard of the place if Anna Quindlen had not taken us there in several of her newspaper columns. The center, run by Roman Catholic nuns, is dedicated to children whose families have no addresses, children who move from place to place, children who have found a touch of home at the center. One day, the sisters took the children to the Jersey shore. None of these three- and four-year-olds had ever seen the ocean. They scrambled up the sandy dunes, falling and giggling their way to the top of what must have seemed like mountains. When they got to the top, they could hardly believe their eyes: water as far as they could see—nothing but water, more water than they had ever seen. They slid down the dunes and ran to the ocean's edge. They chased the waves that teased their toes. Then they all went for a picnic in a nearby park. After lunch, they begged to return to the dunes. One little boy named Freddie outran the rest and climbed his way to the top. He looked out, and shouted to the others: "It's still there!"[3]

O child, in your short life, so much has disappeared. You turned around, and everything familiar was gone. In your world, even the ocean could disappear during dinner. We are older and wise enough to know the ocean will still be there when we look again, but we're not so certain about other things. We often find ourselves scrambling up, up the sandy dunes. Everything is shifting around us, and we're trying to find a place that will hold. We're almost afraid to look up for fear that everything familiar will be gone even though we've never moved.

As we look around the landscape of our country and the larger world, we need to acknowledge that many, including ourselves, are scrambling to secure a place, to shore up the shifting sands:

- *Shore up the borders!* Build a barrier to keep out immigrants (at least, those we don't want).
- *Shore up the streets!* Remove the homeless from our neighborhoods. Make us safer by legalizing the death penalty.
- *Shore up the family!* Pass the "Defense of Marriage Act" to protect traditional values.
- *Shore up the church!* Return to tradition. Silence the voice of feminists. Get back to the Bible.

If we listen carefully to the words and the emotions behind the words, we hear a great deal of fear. Beneath the appeals to scripture and creeds, the voices often sound like the angriest callers to radio talk shows. Personal opinions and deep feelings are equated with what God said. With so many changes swirling around in the culture, the church may seem like the last familiar foundation that we can hold on to.

Not even the safe passage into the third millennium has assuaged our fears. When nothing catastrophic happened as the calendar turned, we all sighed in collective relief from Fiji to Manhattan, and by now we've grown accustomed to writing the strange new date on our checks. Preachers who warned of the endtime and the fires of hell won't have a similar opportunity for another thousand years. Nonetheless, those who never thought of threatening people with hell or an imminent millennial endtime have developed other versions of scary preaching. We often call this "prophetic preaching," in the tradition of Isaiah and Jeremiah.

We stand with Jesus in Nazareth believing that we, too, have been anointed to preach good news to the poor and release to the captives. Looking around us, we see the tragic inequities Amos mourned when he condemned the rich for selling the poor for a pair of shoes. Though the church long ago gave up the communal sharing described in Acts 2 and 4, we're certain that Jesus was serious about the issue of money in his encounter with the rich man. We see the news reports concerning an African immigrant shot forty-one times by white policemen in New York City. We listen to racist conversations in corporate boardrooms; no one can tell us that the tragedy of white racism was overcome in the sixties.

What will people do with such prophetic preaching? Calls for radical change may only increase the uncertainty many are experiencing. Such a fearful analysis—even when it is accurate—will be tuned out completely. What do men do when they sense "that the old givens of white, male, Western, colonial advantage no longer hold"?[4] What do longtime church members do when they suspect that the word *inclusive* doesn't include them? How do blue-collar workers feel about welcoming immigrants into the church when the workers lose their jobs or their company relocates to Mexico?

One response is to try to avoid fearful changes: keep things the way they have been, sing the familiar hymns, stay clear of shifting sand. This is especially true when the call to transformation means a change in our way of life or when the "new alternative text and its redescription of reality" is controversial. A clergywoman who interviewed to be associate pastor in a large congregation was told, "We don't preach about controversial subjects from the pulpit. People want something else from worship." We'll have to cut out major portions of the Bible if we want to avoid controversy in our preaching. And if we do succeed in avoiding all conflict and controversy, the fears won't go away.

"Do not be afraid." Before the news of the Resurrection, this was the word spoken to the women who had come to the tomb in the early hours of morning. They heard the words first from the angel and later from Jesus himself as they ran toward Galilee, but that wasn't the first time those words were said. "Do not be afraid," the angel Gabriel said to Mary. "Do not be afraid," said an angel to startled shepherds sitting under the night sky. "Do not be afraid," Jesus said to disciples on the turbulent sea. "Do not be afraid"—over and over as though no one heard it the first time. Fear is very real in the Gospels from the Annunciation to the Resurrection. The words "Do not be afraid" speak to this reality—fear is neither denied nor covered up. Jesus took fear seriously or he wouldn't have said "Do not be afraid" so often. Jesus knew that his words and actions brought fear as well as assurance. Poet Mary Oliver envisions this fear in the disciples' eyes after Jesus calmed the storm at sea. When the waves died down the disciples could hardly look at him, for Jesus was

> tender and luminous and demanding
> as he always was—
> a thousand times more frightening
> than the killer sea.[5]

Naming the Fears Aloud

If our preaching denies the fear, where will people go with their fears: the fear that everything is changing, the fear of those who are different, the fear that others count more than they do, the fear that God himself is no longer Himself? Fear unnamed does not go away. It lingers inside. It turns inward as depression or outward as verbal and physical violence. Transformation cannot happen if fears are discounted or denied. Those of us who preach are called to name the fears we feel inside ourselves and in those around us. We need to acknowledge that angry outbursts and bravado may mask a deep fear or pain that no one dares to admit. As Larry Rasmussen says, "We are more like those largest dinosaurs whose brains were so far from their tails that the pain of injury only registered some while later. They went on grazing, unfazed, until the pain from their trailing parts finally traveled the many circuits to the head."[6]

At least the women at the tomb dared to tremble in fear and the disciples were not too embarrassed to be terrified: "Save *us*, Lord; we are perishing!" (Matt. 8:25 NASB). Though we are afraid, we must speak. We are not dinosaurs, after all, and the pain has begun to register. We hear it in hospital rooms and in our counseling with people. We see it in the faces of the young and the old. We hear it as someone unlocks three bolts to let us in their front door. We see it in the wooden crosses on the hillside overlooking Columbine High School. The sand is shifting under our feet, and we're afraid there isn't any place that will hold.

Solid Rock and Changing Stones

We long to know that something is still there as the familiar is fading away. We want a mighty fortress, a rock strong enough to hold us while the landscape of our lives is changing. If only we had such rock-solid certainty—about our lives, our beliefs, our future—then we wouldn't be so afraid. Yet certainty can also close the door to possibility. It may help to discover that the "solid" stones in scripture were often not as solid as they seemed. Though this may sound like yet another reason for fear, it can be a source of comfort and encouragement. When we turn to the Bible, we discover that hope didn't always rest on a mighty rock; indeed, hope often came only when the stone was toppled or transformed. The ambivalent stones of scripture can be transformative teachers.

When Israel crossed over the Jordan into the promised land, Joshua commanded twelve men to carry stones from the river to set up a memorial to God's saving acts. The stones set up at Gilgal would be a reminder to the children's children. Such stones are important, calling to mind the Exodus and the covenant long after the sea and Sinai were out of view. We must bring the stones from the river and set them up as markers for the journey: "When your children ask their parents in time to come, 'What do these stones mean?' then you shall let your children know, 'Israel crossed over the Jordan here on dry ground' " (Josh. 4:21-22).

The image of the stone was important to Jesus also. He urged people to build their faith upon the rock rather than shifting sand. He changed Simon's name to Peter, the rock; in Matthew 16:18, he added, "on this rock I will build my church." Whether Jesus meant Peter himself as head of the church or Peter's confession of faith, the church was to be built upon a rock.

But stones don't stay put. Scripture's stones offer an ambivalent image. Sometimes they are the solid alternative to shifting sand, the only foundation on which to build the church, but at other times, stones become rigid, building walls to shut others out. Stones themselves become the focus of worship that lock God outside. Stones become weapons of judgment that can be used to threaten a woman accused of adultery or to kill the prophets sent by God. When Jesus died, a large stone was put in front of the tomb—not as the solid foundation of a new movement, but as a sign of the movement's end, of finality and death. "Who will roll away the stone for us?" (Mark 16:3). That stone could not bring forth life and hope. Do not trust that stone! It had to be rolled away, turned aside to make way for something completely unexpected. This will sometimes be true of tradition's stones, even when such thoughts terrify us.

"Do not be afraid," said the angel. The transformation celebrated in the Magnificat won't happen without controversy. In some people, such transformation elicits more than a little trembling as worlds are turned upside down, but for many, the song gives life and reason for hope. The transformation manifest in the odd community drawn together by Jesus will cause fear and condemnation now even as it did centuries ago, but those invited for the first time will rejoice and be glad. It was Jesus' strong promise that transformation would go on after the resurrection:

> I will not leave you orphaned, I am coming to you. . . . I have said these things to you while I am still with you. But the Advocate, the Holy Spirit, whom the Father will send in my name, will teach you everything, and remind you of all that I have said to you. Peace I leave with you; my peace I give to you. I do not give to you as the world gives. Do not let your hearts be troubled, and do not let them be afraid. (John 14:18, 25-27)

The same Spirit that anointed Jesus continues to anoint us to proclaim words of transformation. Such transformational preaching will take resistance and fear seriously. Though the word, whispered or shouted by the Spirit, may bring disruption and confusion, the Spirit has the power to transform the stones and bring life where the rock had been.

Shaping Our Preaching for Transformation

The chapters that follow trace the image of the stone through scripture, honoring the solid witness of tradition and discerning where the Spirit is calling for transformation. Chapter 1, "Grounded in Grace," begins the journey with God's grace as the necessary foundation for transformative preaching. This chapter acknowledges that many people have yet to experience the assurance of God's grace—even people who are lifelong church members. Without this grounding in grace, the call to transformation becomes another burden, something we try to do by ourselves in order to earn God's favor.

Chapter 2 moves on and borrows words from John the Baptist: "Children from Stones: Shaping New Communities." This chapter seeks tangible ways to reshape Christian communities in light of the Spirit's vivifying capacity to bring stones to life. The preacher reaches out to those who have been shut out of the church, but remains attentive to insiders who feel excluded by the change.

Chapter 3, "Testing What Is Written in Stone," confronts the dangers of traditions grown rigid. This chapter heeds Jesus' call for us to be scribes trained for the kingdom of heaven, bringing out of faith's household not only what is old, but also what is new. "Bearing the Hard Words" is the focus of chapter 4. It takes up the difficult task of preaching words that are hard both to hear and to speak. The growing gap between rich and poor will be a particular example of bearing such hard words. Chapter 5, "Splashing, Bursting Against the Stone," considers preaching over time. Transformation doesn't happen all at once but takes careful planning. The preacher is attentive to resistance and is intentional about moving through resistance to a place of new life.

Finally, chapter 6 claims the image of "living stones" in 1 Peter 2. The stones of death are transformed into living stones: individual lives, including the life of the preacher, are reborn, and communities are reshaped into the Body of Christ. Joshua's stones are remembered not only as monuments to the past, but as stones come to life in this present hour.

> The Church of Christ, in every age
> beset by change but Spirit-led,
> must claim and test its heritage
> and keep on rising from the dead.[7]

SERMON:
TRANSFORMING THE STONE

Matthew 28:1-10

And suddenly there was a great earthquake; for an angel of the Lord, descending from heaven, came and rolled back the stone and sat on it. (Matt. 28:2)

I've heard this Easter gospel many times, but this year I was caught off guard by the angel sitting on the stone. I remembered the angel. All four Gospel writers talk about angels—or at least someone dressed in white—but only Matthew draws this particular picture: "an angel of the Lord, descending from heaven, came and rolled back the stone and sat on it." Can you see it? The angel rolled back the stone and sat on it! Sat right down as though the stone were a bench in the park or the cemetery. I can almost hear the angel laughing and saying, "Do you see this stone? This great stone was rolled in place to close the tomb. This stone not only closed the tomb but also was sealed by soldiers sent on Pilate's authority. This great stone was a sign of finality, earthly authority, power, and death. Look! I'm sitting on the stone, and the tomb is empty!"

Only Matthew draws this particular picture of the angel sitting on the stone. Some people are troubled by this, by the differences among the resurrection stories in the four Gospels. We can be so troubled that we try to make all the stories the same, discounting the differences. But what if we stopped being troubled long enough to pay attention to what is distinct in each story? New Testament scholar N. T. Wright encourages us in that direction: "This is what eyewitness testimony looks and sounds like.... *The surface discrepancies do not mean that nothing happened; rather, they mean that the witnesses have not been in collusion.*"[8]

Did you ever think of the Easter stories that way? If the early Christian community wanted to *prove* the Resurrection as historical fact, they surely would have chosen *one* Easter story as "true" and tossed the others out, or they would have merged all four stories into one story. Instead, they left all four in as though to say, "Pay attention! Listen for what is different, even odd. Each of them has something very important to say."

"Don't miss the angel sitting on the stone!" says Matthew. What does this angel sitting on the great stone of death want to teach us? "Do not be afraid," for starters. That's the word the angel spoke to Mary Magdalene and the other Mary that first Easter morning. The ground was shaking. The guards were shaking. You may be shaking, too, but do not be afraid. The angel sitting on the stone didn't stop there: "I know that you are looking for Jesus who was crucified. He is not here; for he has been raised, as he said. Come, see the place where he lay" (Matt. 28:5-6).

Something strange happens in this story—or perhaps it's strange that something *doesn't* happen. Jesus doesn't come walking out of the tomb when the angel rolls back the stone. Jesus was already gone. "He is not here," the angel said. Resurrection had already happened. The angel didn't roll away the stone to set Jesus free—Jesus was already gone, headed for Galilee. The angel rolled away the stone so the women could see what had already happened. When they saw and heard, the women ran off shaking with fear, but also laughing, singing, shouting, embracing—whatever you do when you're filled with great joy.

As far as we know, the angel was still sitting on the stone when Jesus met the women on the road. Maybe the angel sat there until the guards awoke. Those soldiers who had been sent to guard the dead had become like the dead themselves. If the angel spoke, would they listen? Or would they believe only in what they had known: the strength of their swords, the power of Rome, the rule of fear, the keeping of good order, and the protection of the status quo. Could they hear that word, "Do not be afraid"? Or would they try to push the angel off and set the stone back in place?

We'll never know, for the story doesn't stay at the tomb. Before the guards woke up, before the women got to Galilee, Jesus appeared to them on the road. "Do not be afraid," he said, as though he knew they needed to hear it again. It's not easy to believe in the power of life over death. Indeed, Easter Sunday can be the hardest day of the church year for us. The birth of the baby Jesus at Christmas is easier to comprehend than the grown-up Jesus rising from the dead. But the baby would have been forgotten if Jesus hadn't risen. Jesus might have been remembered as a wise teacher or a peasant revolutionary of the first century, but Easter transforms memory into presence. I can't explain how that is possible anymore than I can explain the creation of the world. I know from my years as a parish pastor that Easter can be the hardest day of all. "Do not be afraid." That was the angel's word. It is also Jesus' word to us on this Easter day, for he knows we need to hear it again and again.

What else does the angel sitting on the stone want us to know? Don't stay here at the place of death! You won't see Jesus by staring where the stone had been. Maybe that's why the angel sat on it: to direct our attention elsewhere! No amount of searching will reveal Jesus in the empty tomb. The women who came to the tomb didn't see Jesus there; Jesus didn't come walking out of the tomb, leaving his grave clothes behind. New Testament scholar Luke Johnson reminds us that the resurrection of Jesus is not resuscitation from clinical death. In John's Gospel, Jesus raised Lazarus from death. Lazarus did come walking out of the tomb: he had been resuscitated. He wasn't more alive than he had been before, and he would someday die.[9] But the earliest witnesses bear testimony that Jesus was *transformed*—alive in a new way beyond the limits of time and space. The Gospel accounts move back and forth between pictures of a Jesus who was physically present—eating, touching, talking—and a Jesus who appeared suddenly on the road or in a locked room, not bound by physical limitations. Jesus does not live in their memories; Jesus is present. The angel wants us to see that the stone of death has been rolled away, turned over, transformed into a resurrection pulpit! Jesus is not memory but presence, presence that continues to transform the forces of death all around us. Sometimes when we dare to start walking toward Galilee, we begin to see.

Theologian Delores Williams bears testimony to resurrection's transforming power. Her African American ancestors were carried to America in slave ships named *John the Baptist, Mary, Justice,* and *Jesus.* When they heard stories from the Bible, they began to find their own story there, even when it was read by their white masters. They saw Jesus led off with his hands tied behind his back, they saw him whipped as they had been whipped, they saw him nailed to the cross though he had done nothing wrong, and they heard the amazing news that God raised him up forever, that the principalities and powers of this world could not keep him down. Delores Williams's ancestors had to transform the names written on the slave ships: *John the Baptist, Mary, Justice, Jesus*—those names had to be turned upside down and inside out. They had to roll away the master's stone and sit on it! "From this centuries-long re-imaging of Jesus emerged a beautiful, redemptive Black liberation theology."[10] They were on their way to Galilee.

Not long ago I took my preaching class to the South Bronx, to Transfiguration Lutheran Church. Pastor Heidi Neumark introduced the neighborhood to us by showing slides of the blocks surrounding the church. We watched as pictures of abandoned apartment buildings gutted by fires flashed on the sanctuary wall; we saw rubble, broken glass, crack vials, and trash. Such images have often appeared on television when politicians venture into the South Bronx for photo opportunities, promising to end "urban blight." The newest building was a shiny prison topped with razor wire, a prison for youth ages ten to sixteen—right across from the junior high. Mingled with these scenes were pictures of children, their faces alive with hope, laughing, lighting altar candles, gathering at the baptismal font, learning to read in the church's after-school program. We saw pictures of mothers meeting together, learning how to fight for their community schools. Imagine if the city and state spent $86,000 each year to keep a child in school—that's what it costs to keep a young person in the brand new razor-topped prison!

But the slides didn't allow us to stay with the laughter of children or the activist mothers for long. Soon we were back on the streets looking at pictures of the shrines painted on the sides of buildings—larger than life faces of young people who died too soon, gunned down on the streets not far from the church. Picture after picture after picture, until we could not bear another. The faces were drawn with love and care and words were written in bold colors on the cinder block: "We will never forget you, Richie." Flowers and candles marked each shrine, brightly painted gravestones rising from the sidewalks. We sat in the darkened sanctuary, overwhelmed with death.

But death was not the final word. As we left the church, Pastor Neumark led us through the front double doors, then asked us to stop and turn around. The doors, once covered with graffiti, had been transformed into gospel doors by youth of the parish. Almost every week, teenage artists paint a new scene, their interpretation of God's good news for their community. I wish you could have seen the painting on those doors! On the left-hand door, a young boy had opened up a fire hydrant—a New York City ritual on stifling summer days. Water was gushing out in a cooling stream that flowed in a wide arc from one door to the other. When it reached the right side, the water splashed into the baptismal font, making one continuous stream from the font to the street and back again. Beneath the flowing water, a table was set: a loaf of bread and a cup of wine, along with a whole roasted chicken and a quart of milk—sacraments of life in the midst of the city. I knew we were in the South Bronx. The sign on the corner said Prospect Avenue and 156th Street, but we had come to Galilee. Jesus was there in the doorway, very much alive. As usual, he had gotten there ahead of us.

And off to the side I thought I saw an angel sitting on a stone.

CHAPTER ONE

Grounded in Grace

Where does transformation begin? Where did Mary's song begin, that song of change so profound of a world turned upside down? She sang in past tense as though transformation had already taken place: "[God] has brought down the powerful from their thrones, and lifted up the lowly; he has filled the hungry with good things, and sent the rich away empty" (Luke 1:52-53). This world-shaking song began in the Spirit-filled imagination of Mary's heart. She sang as though this transformation had already taken place—though Rome still ruled the world and Emperor Augustus was still on the throne.

Mary's song was a response to God's grace breaking into her life in unexpected ways: "My soul magnifies the Lord . . . for he has looked with favor on the lowliness of his servant" (Luke 1:47-48). She could never have predicted any of this: *God has regarded me with favor—no matter what others may think of me or what I may think of myself. God has come to me as I am—not as I should be or as I might become.* Mary's experience of grace did not come from either the conviction of her own sinfulness or a call to repentance. She was not scared into transformation, nor was she threatened, coerced, or convinced of her own pridefulness:

> [Feminist thinkers] have shown how male theological perspectives have dominated understandings of sin as pride and rebellion against God and have failed to

> attend to the sin of those who are powerless, who lack agency, selfhood, and responsibility, who have suffered violence and abuse. . . . Sin is understood, in a feminist perspective, as the breaking of relationship with both God and with human beings that can take the form of weakness as well as pride.[1]

Grace comes to Mary in her lowliness, in what the world could surely perceive as weakness. Mary's song of transformation is grounded in her deep assurance of God's grace, of God's deep regard for her. Throughout the history of Christian communities, other voices have often dominated: voices preaching transformation through fear of damnation or the conviction of people's sinful state. According to these voices, transformation cannot happen until a person repents. This seems to be what Jesus is saying in his first public words in Mark's Gospel: "Now after John was arrested, Jesus came to Galilee, proclaiming the good news of God, and saying, 'The time is fulfilled, and the kingdom of God has come near; repent, and believe in the good news' " (Mark 1:14-15).

But *repent* was not Jesus' first word. Before repentance, Jesus proclaims that "the kingdom of God has come near." Something new was breaking in. The rest of Mark and the other Gospels flesh out Jesus' vision of God's commonwealth. Repentance belongs to this vision, but it is not where Jesus began. Repentance becomes possible when God's grace comes near us. It is the assurance of grace that provides the ground for transformation. From that grounding, the preacher can move on to call for repentance, to urge new behavior or to empower people to risk radical social change—but the starting point is the good news that God's grace has come near.

For many people this grounding in grace is not a reality. Years ago a pastor colleague told me a story about a man in the congregation he served. This man had been a member of the congregation since childhood and had served as treasurer for almost thirty years. But he never came to communion because he didn't feel worthy. He worshiped week after week in a Lutheran church that was centered in the good news of God's free gift of grace, yet he couldn't believe this grace embraced him. This might seem to be an isolated and anachronistic tale in a culture where people seem impressed with their own sense of self, where *sin* has almost disappeared from our common vocabulary, but a brief glance at any list of bestselling books reveals an obsession with self-improvement: getting richer, getting thinner, getting spiritual—that is, becoming someone other than who I am. How can a theological word that may seem far off come near?

Translating a Big Theological Word into Particularities

Grace must take on the flesh of everyday life even as "the Word became flesh and dwelt among us" (John 1:14 NKJV). Grace cannot be a generalized theological concept but must have the specificity that says, "This word is for me." Such preaching calls for attentive listening to both scripture text and community text. It means paying attention to spoken and unspoken stories and bringing them into the communal space of worship and preaching:

- How do people talk about their work? What inadequacies rise to the surface of conversation or lie just beneath the surface in silence? How can the preacher describe in concrete language the fear of being downsized or minimized or the frantic obsession with work never finished, of goals never reached?
- What shame have people carried from year to year? How can that sense of shame find words in a sermon without breaking someone's confidence?

- What stories speak the agony of "not good enough": never chosen for the team, never as good as my sister or brother, never a good enough mother or father, never as good as the other members of this congregation?
- How can the promise of God's grace and acceptance overcome messages from a culture that insists on making, earning, or deserving this grace and acceptance?

How can grace be as tangible as its absence? This is a question not only for those who have been treated as outsiders, but also for those who have always been part of the church. What is needed to get the older brother to come inside to eat and dance with the long-lost prodigal? (Perhaps his mother will have to leave the house and find words that have never been spoken before.) Homiletics professor William Muehl often challenged students at Yale Divinity School by saying, "Don't talk to me about grace—show me grace!"

Frank Thomas, parish pastor and writer, encourages preachers to help people move beyond cognitive understanding to *experiencing* the assurance of grace. He writes about a funeral sermon he heard about secondhand. It was a sermon so powerful that the storyteller remembered it almost word-for-word seventy years later! Responding to that sermon after it was retold, Thomas writes:

> In the midst of profound anguish and suffering, the African American preacher sought not to give answers to the problem of suffering and evil in life, but to help people experience the assurance of grace in God. The preacher gave assurance to the people that God was with them, in and through the suffering, and would ultimately liberate them from the suffering. The point was not abstract answers to suffering and evil, . . . but an experience of the transforming, sustaining, and saving power of God in the midst of suffering and evil.[2]

Like Mary centuries before him, this unnamed preacher sang the experience of God's grace even while the emperor was still on the throne.

The preacher's own life can depict the specificity of grace (as long as the preacher isn't always the hero!). In a teaching sermon about the biblical figure *Sophia*, the female personification of Wisdom, Ron Allen recalls a painful experience from his own childhood. Born with a large birthmark on his face, he learned to live with stares from adults and other children. Sometimes he almost forgot about how he looked—but not always:

> When I was about eight, I was with some neighborhood kids. We were building a dam across a drainage ditch down the block. A new kid came up, looked me full in the face, and cried out, "That's the ugliest thing I've ever seen."
>
> I was crushed. I climbed out of the ditch and ran home into the kitchen, where my mother wrapped my sobbing body in her apron. She was there. For me. She mediated God's presence for me. That day, I called her Mother. Today, I might call her *Sophia*.[3]

Sermons need to speak to a variety of specific life situations within the congregation. Attentive listening to people in the parish and the larger community will reveal deep wounds that have never healed and shame that has been covered over. Some of these wounds are in the preacher's own life. Though preaching must never betray confidences, the stories and images of the sermon can touch the lives of particular people when chosen with their faces and voices in mind. It's important to take inventory of our preaching over time to discern those we may have missed along the way:

- Has grace touched those who live with traumatic memories of childhood rejection and feel they will never be accepted or loved?

- Has grace reached the widow who feels her life is over and that God's favor has passed her by? Does preaching about "family ministry" leave her out completely?
- Has grace knocked at the door of the man ashamed of his divorce? Does he know that Jesus' hard words about divorce are followed by his invitation to the children to come to him? Has he been invited to climb up into Jesus' lap?
- Has grace honored the pain of the fifteen-year-old boy who doesn't fit into any group at school? Can his story be told through a recent movie or television show without making him feel exposed?
- Has grace walked with the man who depends on his job for his sense of worth and is never satisfied that he's done enough?
- Has grace broken through racist words and actions that demean and oppress men, women, and children? How can this word break through to those who have suffered from racial discrimination? How can this word transform the minds and hearts of those who are racists, those who need God's grace to outgrow their frantic efforts to build themselves up by keeping others down?

The Diverse Pictures of Grace in Scripture

Preaching grace is enfleshed by words and pictures as diverse as the images of scripture. Grace cannot be limited to one text alone or confined to any one formulation. *Justification by grace through faith* (Rom. 3:24; Gal. 2:16) is a life-giving word, but it is not God's only way of speaking. We need to be mindful of dangerous dualisms that divide scripture too neatly into Law and Gospel, especially when that division sees Law in the Old Testament and Gospel in the New. Grace permeates the pages of the Bible from the very beginning. Joseph Sittler reminds us of the amplitude of grace when he says, "What I am appealing for is an understanding of grace that has the magnitude of the doctrine of the Holy Trinity. The grace of God is not simply a holy hypodermic whereby my sins are forgiven. It is the whole giftedness of life, the wonder of life, which causes me to ask questions that transcend the moment."[4]

The pages of the Bible hum with God's grace, from the doxology of the Genesis creation story to the new heaven and the new earth of Revelation, from the incarnate love of Jesus to the indwelling of the Holy Spirit. Preaching draws upon this deep well of images, stories, songs, and visions to reach people where they live, perhaps to surprise them with pictures of grace that they'd never seen before:

- *Grace is hearing your name attached to God's name:* "I have called you by name, you are mine" (Isa. 43:1*b*).
- *Grace is being welcomed home after rebellions too numerous to count:* "How can I give you up, Ephraim? How can I hand you over, O Israel? . . . My heart recoils within me; my compassion grows warm and tender. I will not execute my fierce anger; I will not again destroy Ephraim; for I am God and no mortal, the Holy One in your midst, and I will not come in wrath" (Hos. 11:8-9).
- *Grace is the assurance of God's presence in the midst of despair and emptiness:* "Where can I go

from your spirit? Or where can I flee from your presence? If I ascend to heaven, you are there; if I make my bed in Sheol, you are there. If I take the wings of the morning and settle at the farthest limits of the sea, even there your hand shall lead me, and your right hand shall hold me fast" (Ps. 139:7-10).

- *Grace is a word of healing deeper than disease:* In Luke 13 Jesus heals a woman who had been bent over for eighteen years. His first words to her were, "Woman, you are set free from your ailment." Only after that did Jesus touch her and cure her bent-down body.
- *Grace is a gift so unexpected it interrupts our desperate attempts to hide our sinfulness and our frantic efforts to win God's favor:* "For there is no distinction, since all have sinned and fall short of the glory of God; they are now justified by his grace as a gift, through the redemption that is in Christ Jesus" (Rom. 3:22*b*-24).

Beyond Scripture: Other Sources for Images of Grace

In addition to the pictures of grace in scripture, the preacher searches the pages of his or her own life, the congregation, the larger community, literature, newspaper, and film. The preacher asks the question poets ask when they are searching for metaphors: "What is this like?" What have people seen and heard that can make grace real? Like the priest in Anne Lamott's book *Traveling Mercies*, the preacher looks everywhere for an image that might work: "I guess it's like discovering you're on the shelf of a pawnshop, dusty and forgotten and maybe not worth very much. But Jesus comes in and tells the pawnbroker, 'I'll take her place on the shelf. Let her go outside again.' "[5] Grace is an African American teenager saying "I am somebody" and knowing it's true in spite of what others may have said. Grace is clean wash hanging on the line, blowing in the summer wind. Grace is your mother running to embrace you when you've been lost in the department store for what seemed like forever. Grace is a wound that begins to heal. Grace is ______. The preacher fills in the blank with pictures that will carry meaning for the people in a particular congregation.

The metaphors for grace are born in the places where people live. These metaphors are biblical and congregational—as specific as each person sitting in the sanctuary. Generalizations won't do. "My soul magnifies the Lord," Mary sang—*my* soul. This tangible assurance of God's grace is the grounding for transformation. Words become more than words. Mary Oliver reminds us of this mystery when she writes about poems—but we might dare to imagine that she could also be talking about sermons: "For poems are not words, after all, but fires for the cold, ropes let down to the lost, something as necessary as bread in the pockets of the hungry."[6] So may it be when we preach God's word of grace.

SERMON: GRACE FOR THE UNGRACEFUL

Romans 3:19-31 and John 8:31-38

For there is no distinction, since all have sinned and fall short of the glory of God, they are now justified by his grace as a gift, through the redemption that is in Christ Jesus. (Rom. 3:22b-24)

If you have listened to *The Protestant Hour* for a long time, you'll know by now that I grew up on a farm near the little town of Gowrie, Iowa. Even though I now live in New York City—with more people on my block than in that little town—my roots and my memories are deeply set in that Iowa soil. I vividly remember sitting in my parents' car on Saturday nights outside the Gowrie roller skating rink. In the summer, the wooden rink became the place for dances—teen hops, as we called them. I was thirteen, maybe fourteen—still too young to drive, so my parents drove me into town every Saturday night. Though they were a bit uncertain whether dancing was appropriate for Lutherans, they were committed to my happiness. They gladly chauffeured me to the parking lot, then gently convinced me to open the car door. I could hear the rock music pumping through the walls of the roller rink. "You'll have a good time," my mother would say—which she said every time we went through this ritual. I looked for somebody I knew going toward the door so I wouldn't have to walk in alone. Finally, I would get up enough courage to get out of the car and walk toward the sound of the music (but I usually looked back over my shoulder, just in case I could catch my parents before they drove away).

Once inside, I scanned the dim room, looking for my friends so I wouldn't have to stand along the wall all alone. But finding my friends didn't help much because most of them didn't want to stand around. They knew how to dance and they'd dance with each other if no one asked them. The reason for that went back to sixth grade, I told myself. At the beginning of that school year, I had whooping cough and missed six weeks of school. By the time I got back, all my friends had learned to dance, practicing on a big cement platform behind the gymnasium. (To this day, I'm still six weeks behind all the other dancers in my age group.) So the most important thing to me was to find someone else who wouldn't be dancing much. Then the two of us could stand together against the wall, trying to talk to each other over the music and trying to look as though we didn't mind standing still when others were moving. Though I could remember being asked to dance many times, each week was a new struggle: maybe I look worse this week, maybe the person who asked me to dance last week remembers how I danced! I always hoped for a slow song—it had more to do with fear of speed than romance.

I seldom feel more *ungraceful* than when I'm dancing, except perhaps when I'm waiting to see if anyone will ask me to dance. It's always the same kind of emptiness, like standing alone at a crowded party, hearing the laughter all around and being at the edge of lively conversation, but not really part of it. That kind of loneliness feels much worse than being alone in your own room.

This loneliness is not limited to dances when you're thirteen, or to parties. Such loneliness is probably part of our lives at every age. Being asked to dance may seem a silly thing to worry about—a small problem on the world's stage, insignificant beside the tragedies faced daily by millions of people. But it may be the experiences we discount or belittle that become our teachers, pointing to deeper places within. I had that experience not long ago when I read a poem in Gerhard Frost's book *Seasons of a Lifetime*. He takes us back to the fourth grade, opening the poem with these words:

> You know, Mom,
> your world is pretty nice
> compared to going out to recess.[7]

Do you remember the terror recess can hold for a child? In the classroom everybody has a place—a desk, a table, a nursery-rhyme square on the floor—but at recess, you're on your own. Friends huddle in groups laughing. Teams are chosen for softball, and someone is always picked last or not at all. Recess can be the most ungraceful time of all. On the subway, I watch sixteen-year-old boys in baggy pants too short to be jeans and too long to be shorts, their baseball caps worn backwards, their sneakers in the $100 range. They're at recess on the A train, wearing the right brands, hoping somebody will choose them for the team, and wondering if the girls at the far end of the car would ever dance with them.

From the day of birth, when someone cut the umbilical cord that connected us to our mother, life has been marked by separation. Some theologians call this separation "alienation" or "estrangement"—a sense of being cut off from the very source of life. We experience this separation on a human scale within our families, with those people we love most. We also experience separation from God. This deep separation is the root of sin, even though we tend to think of *sins*—plural. Each of us could probably make a list of sins, and our lists would include broken commandments, taboos, and other specific wrongdoings. Such things, however, are signs of the fundamental separation from the source of life, the one Christians call God. I do not doubt that others find different names; I also do not doubt that they, too, are searching for a reunion.

This search for reunion is at the heart of Reformation Sunday. Though there may have been a time when this day applauded the Protestant break with Rome, it should no longer be a day to celebrate separation. At the heart of this day is the promise of an end to our separation: it is the good news of reunion with God. This reunion is a word of grace for the ungraceful. The Reformation text from John's Gospel speaks Jesus' powerful word about being set free. Alongside this Gospel text is Paul's letter to the Romans: "Everyone has sinned and is far away from God's saving presence" (3:23 TEV).

Everyone. I do what I know is wrong, and I fail to do what I know is right. For Paul, it is the Law that makes us aware of our deep separation from God, "for through the law comes the knowledge of sin." This is the case whether we're speaking of God's commandments given on Sinai or laws written by human hands. The minute we think we've succeeded in honoring our parents, we remember that we've spoken hurtful words about someone else. I feel confident that I haven't stolen anything, but then I remember how much I covet what somebody else has, whether it's money or a gift for dancing. Something inside keeps saying, *I'll never be good enough. I'll never be a good enough parent. I'll never be a good enough pastor.* We'll never be good enough to one another (or to ourselves, for that matter). We hear the laughter and noise of existence all around us, wondering still if we will ever feel at home.

Paul doesn't stop with the law or with the pervasive power of sin. He goes on: "Everyone has sinned and is far away from God's saving presence. But by the free gift of God's grace all are put right with him through Christ Jesus, who sets them free" (Rom. 3:23-24 TEV). These were the words that captured Martin Luther's heart as he struggled alone in his study, words that seemed to be caught in a shaft of sunlight streaming through the leaded window panes. Luther had tried all his life to be at peace with God—to pray enough, to sacrifice enough, to obey enough, to do enough, to be enough; he didn't even dare to imagine that God would ask him to dance. But it happened that day in the tower study: Luther experienced God's grace for the ungraceful. This is God's unexpected gift for those who stand against the wall waiting to be asked and for those moving so fast they haven't noticed that anything's missing.

The Bible proclaims that we are *saved* by God's grace—and the word "saved" is even harder for us than grace!

It sounds too old-fashioned somehow, too outmoded—too tied to that other word we don't like, "guilt." Nevertheless, our distaste for the word "saved" isn't so different from the protestations of those who argued with Jesus in John's Gospel. "If you continue in my word," Jesus said, "you are truly my disciples; and you will know the truth, and the truth will make you free" (8:31-32). The religious leaders protested, saying, "We are descendants of Abraham and have never been slaves to anyone. What do you mean by saying, 'You will be made free'?" (John 8:33). That is, "*We* don't need to be saved. We've always been part of the chosen people." Or we've always been church members. Or we don't feel burdened by guilt—why do we need to be set free? Our modern arguments don't sound very new. We're not the first generation to insist that we don't need to be set free! We may argue against the notion of *original sin*, but our arguments will hardly be original!

We're not the first generation to sense deep estrangement—separation from ourselves, from one another, and from Something or Someone beyond ourselves. We're not the first, but our sense of separation may be more acute than our ancestors'. For the givens that connected people to one another are no longer givens: the continuity of growing up in the same community as our parents and grandparents, knowing life will be better for our children than for ourselves, trusting that hard work for the company will ensure lifetime employment—you can add your own experience to the long list of stabilities that have disappeared. It's harder and harder to find security in the place we live (since we might be moving next year) or in our job (since we might lose it next month) or in our church (since they introduced the new hymnal and nothing is the way we remember). Our sense of separation is real, even if we're uncomfortable with the notion of "being saved."

The longing for reunion does not go away. The fear of not being good enough keeps nagging us even when we succeed, even when we remember that last week someone asked us to dance. Look at a list of bestselling books in this country, and you'll find several of the top ten nonfiction books trying to help us get thin, stay thin, make money, invest money, learn how to talk to each other, and discover how to love enough but not too much. What must I do to overcome my ungracefulness? Nothing.

I know that's hard to sell and hard to believe, but this is the heart of the gospel promise. It is a promise of separation overcome, a promise of being made right with God, a promise of reunion. Years ago theologian Paul Tillich preached about this surprising reunion. His language sounds unbiblical to some, too amorphous for others, and has too little to say about Jesus for many—indeed, he doesn't even use the word "God." Tillich, however, is trying to get through to us, to help us see the grace that we can no longer even imagine, the grace we think we don't need because we have it all—grace meant for another generation, but not our own. "Grace strikes us when we are in great pain and restlessness. It strikes us when we walk through the dark valley of a meaningless and empty life. . . . It strikes us when, year after year, the longed-for perfection of life does not appear."[8]

You and I can add our own experiences to his—and we ought not be hesitant to include the little things that seem silly, like waiting to be asked to dance or worrying over recess. These small memories alert us to deeper needs or harder confessions that we've been afraid to admit to anyone, including ourselves. It is here, in these empty spaces or in places filled with frantic busyness, that grace breaks in, like a voice telling us:

> "You are accepted. *You are accepted,* accepted by that which is greater than you, and the name of which you

> do not know. Do not ask for the name now; perhaps you will find it later. Do not try to do anything now; perhaps later you will do much. Do not seek anything, do not perform anything; do not intend anything. *Simply accept the fact that you are accepted!*" If that happens to us, we experience grace.
>
> We experience moments in which we accept ourselves, because we feel that we have been accepted by that which is greater than we.[9]

Someone has asked us to dance, and we don't have to worry about knowing the steps. This is grace for the ungraceful. Can you and I quiet the protests of our minds long enough to hear this deep word of acceptance? Can we forget that we didn't "need to be saved"? Can I stop clinging to the wall, feeling awkward and embarrassed about who I am? Let me admit something to you: I'm *still* ungraceful, but God has asked me to dance.

"You will know the truth," said Jesus, "and the truth will make you free." *"But I'm already free. I don't need to—"*

Shhhh, says Jesus. Come and dance. Come and dance.

SERMON: TOUCHING THE WOUNDS

John 20:19-31

Then [Jesus] said to Thomas, "Put your finger here and see my hands. Reach out your hand and put it in my side. Do not doubt but believe." (John 20:27)

It seems much too early for Easter to be over—all of April stretching ahead of us with Easter already a week old. The relatives, if they came for Easter dinner, have all gone home, and the last egg has been found under the sofa cushion in the living room. So here we are: waiting. But not quite sure what we're waiting for. Perhaps we are waiting for spring to break through the hard ground, for the planting season to begin, for school to be over. Or to see if Easter made any difference to us or anybody else. We've hung the good suits back in the closet and set the wilted lilies out on the back steps. We've closed the door, and now, we wait.

It wasn't so different in Jerusalem. Friday and Saturday had passed. Sunday had come, and with the dawn came the unexpected—indeed, unbelievable—news that Jesus had risen from the dead. (It was the same word the preacher brought us a week ago when the church was filled and we sat listening in our good suits.) The disciples who gathered in the room had heard the news but hadn't seen anything to confirm it, so they closed the door and locked it. And they waited. Some, no doubt, wondered if it was time to go home, to get back to whatever they had been doing before all of this happened. To pick up the pieces and start over. But for now, they waited, not quite sure what they were waiting for.

We know the story: their waiting paid off. Without knocking or unlocking the door, Jesus Christ appeared in their midst saying, "Peace be with you." We get little evidence of the disciples' reaction—just Jesus' simple greeting, "Peace be with you"—as though he were waiting for the liturgical response, "And also with you." Then something rather strange happened. This same Jesus who had appeared to Mary Magdalene in the garden and told her not to hold him, now invites the disciples to look at his scarred hands and side. Eight days later, Jesus again comes into the room without opening the door and invites Thomas to touch him. To place his fingers in the print of the nails. To put his hand in Jesus' wounded side.

Now this is odd; it's convincing, but strange just the

same. I come to this part of the story longing to ask questions children dare to ask before they know better. If God raised Jesus from the dead, why didn't God fix him up? Why does Jesus have scars so deep you could feel the print of the nails?

We quickly give the child answers: "This is how the disciples knew for certain it was Jesus." Come now. Mary Magdalene knew simply by hearing Jesus say her name aloud in the garden. In Luke's Gospel two disciples recognized Jesus at the table in Emmaus when he broke bread. There is no mention of wounded hands. Why are there wounds in this story?

Who knows? God knows. Even the child who dares the question knows there is something in the scars. Something important. As important as Mary hearing her own name in the garden when she was convinced only of Jesus' death. As important as a stranger breaking bread with two disciples at Emmaus—their eyes were opened and they knew it was Jesus. But as soon as they recognized him, Jesus disappeared, leaving them with pieces of broken bread and each other. The scars are not proof—especially for those of us who have never touched them. The scars remain as a witness to the truth.

Why didn't God fix Jesus up? Surely God could have. At times it seems that God did, for Jesus' resurrected body was not limited by time or space. "Do not hold me," Jesus said to Mary, as though his body couldn't be embraced or held or touched. In this story Christ appears inside a locked room without coming through the door, yet this is no ghost! Touch my hands, my side. Touch these wounds, and peace be with you.

What is this story saying to us in our waiting? Many things, no doubt, but there is one thing we dare not overlook: we won't see Jesus unless we see his wounds. The resurrected Christ is forever the wounded Christ—living, but never all fixed up; not bound by death, yet scarred for eternity. People who are deaf or know sign language have a sign for Jesus, and they make the sign many times during worship: the left middle finger touches the right palm, then the right middle finger touches the left palm. When they touch the place they speak without words: Jesus, the one with wounded hands. They bear Jesus' name in their own flesh.

We must touch the places where the wounds are. This isn't the only place where Jesus Christ is revealed, but if we deny the wounds, we will see only a glorified Christ who can go through locked doors, whose only name is victory. The wounded Christ shows us something else: this scarred Jesus meets us *before* we're all fixed up.

- Have you been betrayed by someone you loved or betrayed by a cause you'd given your life to? " 'Behold,' said Jesus, 'one of you will betray me' " (Matt. 26:20).
- Have you been let down by your closest friends or by people who have broken large or small promises without apology? " 'Could you not stay awake with me one hour?' Jesus asked them" (Matt. 26:40).
- Have you been afraid to go on living but also afraid to die? Have you been uncertain whether you had any sense of God's will for your life or anyone else's? " 'Father,' Jesus prayed, 'if you are willing, remove this cup from me' " (Matt. 26:39*a*).
- Have you felt utterly alone, completely abandoned? "Jesus cried out, 'My God, my God, why have you forsaken me?' " (Matt. 27:46*b*).

Touch the palms of your hands. Jesus was wounded long before the cross. His wounds touch the wounded places of our lives: all the betrayals and all the denials—

our own and those made against us. Jesus' birth as a human child marked him with the wounds we all feel as children of earth. Jesus was not a spiritual baby nor did he float over Galilee without touching the ground. "The Word became flesh and dwelt among us," wrote John. Touch the palms of your hands.

Touch the places where the wounds are in your own life and in the lives of others. No one is unscarred by living. You and I have wounds almost too painful to bear, wounds we can't talk about, even with those we love. We will never be all fixed up, not in this life. The wounded Christ comes to us saying, "Peace be with you." You don't have to pretend that you're all right, that everything in your life is fine. Jesus comes to you and me as we are saying, "Peace be with you."

Years ago I saw a play that invited me and the other audience members to end our pretense. In the play Lily Tomlin portrayed all the characters, from Trudy the bag lady to Agnes Angst, a punk rock teenager. Agnes is furious with the world. She dresses to show rebellion against everything and everyone. She rails in anger against her father, the biochemist experimenting with new life forms in the lab. She's disgusted with her grandparents and their plastic-covered living room. When she can no longer stand to be with her parents or her grandparents, she runs away to "The House of Pancakes." There, in the trashcan, she finds a book by G. Gordon Liddy. In his book, *Will*, he claims that human beings have the capacity to do anything they want; they can keep pushing against all the odds. He compared this extraordinary human willpower to holding your hand over a lit candle: "The trick is not to mind it."[10]

As the first act of the play comes to a close, Agnes is alone on stage. She flings defiance at the whole world—her parents, the lab, the plastic-covered furniture, and every other hypocrisy. "I don't mind I was born at the time of the crime known as Watergate. And must've missed out on most things that made America great. *But I don't mind it*... I don't mind that the teenage suicide rate is soaring like Halley's comet. The boy in school that I loved the most died last year of an overdose. But I don't mind it."[11]

Then she bends down to light an imaginary candle. One beam of light focuses on her hand as she speaks: "For life is like that candle flame and we are like Gordon Liddy's hand hovering over it. And it hurts like hell, but the trick is not to mind it."[12] All goes dark and the curtain comes down. In the darkness of the theatre we hear Agnes cry out, "I MIND IT!!"[13] I mind.

Touch the palms of your hands. The word is Jesus, and his word for you and me is, "I mind." I mind your pain and your loneliness, your abandonment and your despair. Don't pretend your pain doesn't matter. Don't wait until you're all fixed up. "Put your finger here in the print of the nails. Place your hand in my side. Do not be faithless, but believing."

My wounded sister, my wounded brother, I mind.

CHAPTER TWO

Children from Stones: Shaping New Communities

Grace changes lives, welcomes prodigals, surprises the self-sufficient, regards the lowly with esteem, blesses the unworthy, and forgives the unforgivable. In her irreverent conversion story, Anne Lamott puts it this way: "I do not at all understand the mystery of grace—only that it meets us where we are but does not leave us where it found us."[1] Grace calls us into a different kind of community. Can preaching help people make the connection between God's grace and the shaping of new communities? Jim Wallis makes this connection in his book *The Call to Conversion:*

> When I was a university student, I was unsuccessfully evangelized by almost every Christian group on campus. My basic response to their preaching was, "How can I believe when I look at the way the church lives?" They answered, "Don't look at the church—look at Jesus."
>
> I now believe that statement is one of the saddest in the history of the church. It puts Jesus on a pedestal apart from the people who name his name. . . . Such thinking is a denial of what is most basic to the gospel: incarnation.[2]

Wallis believes that "forming community has been the social strategy of the Spirit since Pentecost. . . . A good test of any theology of conversion is the kind of community it creates."[3] This new community is so unexpected, so surprising, that John the Baptist portrayed it as stones coming to life: "For I tell you, God is able from these stones to raise up children to Abraham" (Luke 3:8*b*). To some this was a word of promise, but to others, it was surely a threat. Those who claimed that tradition's stones were solid and unchanging were confronted with the possibility that other stones might come to life and be counted as Abraham's children. Christian preaching can interpret this to mean that Abraham and Sarah's descendants have been disenfranchised and replaced by Gentile children born of the new covenant. But such thinking disregards Paul's strong affirmation of God's covenant with Israel in Romans, as well as the testimony of the Old Testament. Ishmael's story is not forgotten, even when Isaac's story becomes the focus. "The narrative knows the 'canonical' story must be presented. That story is an Isaac story. But the text is equally clear that God is well inclined toward Ishmael. The 'other son' is not to be dismissed from the family. The narrative holds us to the tension found so often in this narrative, the tension between the one *elected* and the not-elected one who is *treasured*."[4]

While telling the story of the people of Israel, the Hebrew Scriptures are interwoven with stories of outsiders. Esther's courageous defense of her people, the Jews, shares canonical status with Jonah's reluctant mission to the unchosen Ninevites. The story of Ruth, the Moabite woman, is squeezed into a small space between conquering the Promised Land and forming the nation of Israel. Isaiah the prophet cries out his love for Jerusalem but proclaims God's expansive vision:

> In days to come
> the mountain of the LORD's house
> shall be established as the highest of the mountains,

and shall be raised above the hills;
all the nations shall stream to it. (Isa. 2:2)

The boundaries of God's commonwealth are not set in stone. After Jesus began his public ministry, it soon became clear that the stones were shaking. The strange children predicted by John the Baptist began to gather around Jesus wherever he went. People who had been stepped on like stones underfoot now sat at the table. Jesus picked up John's image when he entered Jerusalem and responded to critics who demanded that he silence the crowds: "I tell you, if these were silent, the stones would shout out" (Luke 19:40).

How Can Our Preaching Move People Toward Jesus' Vision of Community?

For those who have known the tragic wounds of ostracism and oppression, God's word of inclusion and blessing is the bottom line for all preaching. Thomas Hoyt, Jr. is clear about this bottom line for preaching in the African American community: "It is apparent that fundamental to any black biblical hermeneutic are the universal parenthood of God and the concomitant universal kinship of humankind."[5] Any community claiming to believe in God must be shaped by this two-fold understanding: because God is parent of all races, everyone is related whether they like it or not.

Unfortunately, this sacred bottom line runs into human opposition at many turns. This opposition cannot be countered simply by posting big letters on the church bulletin board that say, "ALL ARE WELCOME HERE." Our preaching must be more specific and incarnational than a generic message beside the church doors. Those who have felt the sting of exclusion need to hear God's welcome in ways that honor and respect their particularities. Some of these people will be sitting in the congregation on Sunday mornings, yet may not feel part of the community. Others have never been invited, and the preacher's challenge is to awaken those inside to see through the stained glass windows to those who are still waiting outside the door.

- *People who grew up hearing only words of condemnation from the church:* divorced women and men, gay and lesbian people, persons with disabilities who have been told they are not whole, single people in a "family" church, and teenagers who are convinced that their sexual feelings are sinful. When have you, the preacher, felt excluded?

- *People who live with hidden shame and those who feel their life stories have no place in the church:* alcoholics and addicts, survivors of childhood sexual abuse, those who continue to live with the agony of domestic violence, doubters and agnostics, people who have a mental illness or are affected by someone with a mental illness. What public media (newspaper, movie, television, magazine or book) could touch those who feel ashamed without breaking confidence or embarrassing any person?

- *People who are in a different class than the majority in the congregation:* the woman who sits in the balcony because her clothes aren't "good enough," the man who has been unemployed for six months (but never talks about it), the homeless man who sits in the back or kneels at the altar railing in the middle of the sermon, the single mother whose phone number isn't listed in the directory because she can't afford a phone. How can someone who is living in poverty be fully welcomed within the congregation?

- *People whose race or ethnicity is different from the majority in the congregation:* new immigrants struggling to learn English, Mexican workers who have settled in Iowa towns to work in meat packing plants, Guyanese coming to a predominantly white congregation. Are the stories and images in the sermon as culturally diverse as the people listening? How can the preacher stretch minds and hearts by quoting voices that had been neglected or silenced?

How Can Preaching Help People Move Through Resistance to This New Community?

It's impossible to travel very far in the Gospels without bumping into stories, images, encounters and teachings through which Jesus is shaping a new community. This is a community in which water is thicker than blood, family is redefined, lepers are touched, and outcasts sit at the table. We also don't have to look far to see how threatening this change was to many. There was resistance to Jesus' open table, and such opposition continues in our own time. How can we enter this resistance and help people move through it?

Moving from the familiar to the strange. Dr. James Forbes, senior minister of The Riverside Church in New York City, offers a possible model for moving into and through resistance:

> Years ago, when I was still living in North Carolina, someone said to me, "Brother Forbes, do you think the gospel can be preached by someone who is not Pentecostal?" Well, I wasn't sure, for it was the only preaching I had known, but I imagined that it could

> happen even if I hadn't seen it or heard it. Indeed, I found out some time later that it was so.
>
> After I had moved away from my hometown, someone said to me, "Reverend Forbes, have you ever heard the true gospel from a white preacher?" Well, in theory I knew it had to be true for God doesn't withhold the Spirit from anyone. Though I had my doubts that a white preacher could speak with power, I came to a point in my life where I had to say, "Yes, I've heard it!"
>
> Some time went by, and people began to press upon me the question of the ordination of women. "Could the gospel be preached by a woman even though the holy scriptures bid a woman to keep silence in the church?" I had to ponder this, for it went against what I had known in my own church and there was much resistance from my brother clergy. But I listened to my sisters and before too long I knew the Spirit of God was calling them to preach. Who was I to get in God's way?

Then Dr. Forbes paused. He moved up and down the aisles of the church, stopping now and then to note how people were taking in his words. After a considerable silence, he went on.

> Now, I thought I had been asked the last question about who might be called to bring me the word of the Lord. But I found out I was wrong. A new question has been posed to me and many of you know what it is: "Can gay men and lesbian women be called to preach the word of God?" Oh, I know what the Bible says and I know what my own uneasiness says and I can see that same uneasiness in some of your faces. But I've been wrong before, and the Spirit has been nudging me to get over my uneasiness. Sometimes we forget Jesus' promise—that the Spirit will lead us into all the truth. Well, that must have meant the disciples didn't know it all then, and maybe we don't know it all now.[6]

Dr. Forbes moved from the familiarity of his childhood church to the stranger territory of women's ordination and finally to homosexuality. He made all of these moves within one sermon, but his model could be used for preaching-over-time—being intentional about charting a course that begins on familiar terrain but travels to places that are less familiar and often more frightening.

Moving from points of lesser to greater resistance. A related, but slightly different model for accepting change is beginning at a point of lesser resistance and moving toward a point where resistance is greater. Consider the issue of language, particularly the language of public worship, including preaching. Language has the power to reshape community and to encourage people to hear and see those whose presence has not been fully affirmed. Does the language of hymns, creeds, prayers, and sermons reflect the diversity of the Body of Christ?

The Pentecost vision includes men and women, young and old, menservants and maidservants. It also includes people of every nation—surely this would have meant many races and cultures gathered in Jerusalem. Hearing new language begins to reshape community, but this new language can cause dissonance with what people have known. There will no doubt be stiff resistance if a pastor begins ministry in a congregation by changing the language of the Lord's Prayer to "Our Mother and Father who art in heaven." Liturgical language printed in the worship book is a difficult place to start, and language about God is considered by many to be unchangeable. But sermons aren't printed in a book and are more open to exploration of neglected biblical images as well as images from our own lives. Sermons can be the arena for practicing Pentecost language. Sermons can speak of the significance of being addressed as "Brothers and Sisters" first—then move on to explore female imagery for God. Sermons can help listeners see human beings rather than categories:

> Words that categorize people dehumanize them as well. One such example is references to people by adjectives without nouns. I refer to expressions like "the poor," "the homeless," "the blind." We are speaking about *people in our midst* for whom we are all accountable. They are poor people, homeless people, people who are blind . . . not a lump of unknown, general, convenient groupings of marginalized beings.[7]

Sermons can also awaken people to the negative ways the word *black* is used in the wider culture, and in our worship: black sheep, blackmail, a black mark. On the other hand, *white* is almost always good: Snow White is pure and beautiful, the good guys in Westerns wear white hats, and when we're forgiven we're washed whiter than snow. Several years ago an article in a church magazine described a baptismal service in which the baby was brought to the font dressed in black. At the moment of baptism, the black garment was removed and the baby was submerged for the three-fold washing. The newly baptized child was then dressed in a garment of white: she had "put on Christ." Without thinking, our language and visual images can perpetuate racist stereotypes. Hymnist Brian Wren sings of God's presence not only in light but also in darkness:

> Great, living God, never fully known,
> joyful darkness far beyond our seeing,
> closer yet than breathing,
> everlasting home:
> Hail and Hosanna,
> great, living God![8]

How Can Our Preaching Reach Those Who Feel Left Behind in This Reshaped Community?

Preaching Jesus' vision of community also means being attentive to those who feel there's no longer any room for them. "If these stones can become children to

Abraham and Sarah, who will I be?" At a recent Lutheran churchwide assembly, a bishop came to the microphone at the closing session. He hadn't come to make an amendment or call for a vote, but to ask for a point of personal privilege: "Could we all rise and join in singing 'A Mighty Fortress Is Our God'?" His request didn't come after a particularly divisive session, but out of a deep personal longing. During that assembly, we had sung in Spanish and clapped the rhythms of South African freedom songs, and we had heard new images for God lifted up in prayers. The bishop hadn't heard his heritage lifted up or celebrated in ten days of meetings. He wanted us to sing a song he knew before going home.

No doubt some will say, "That's too bad! We've spent fifteen hundred years singing his songs!" Many at that assembly delighted in the Pentecost diversity of language and music while others, like the bishop, felt the church was moving on without them. How can our preaching remember the bishop and others who feel estranged within the church of their birth? Sermons must reach out not only to the prodigal, but also to the older brother who is standing outside while others are inside feasting and dancing. Many of these elder brothers and sisters are sitting in the pews Sunday after Sunday (and it's not only a matter of age):

- *Farmers and residents of small towns* who hear the church's energy and commitment focused on the cities. A program lifting up the mission of the urban church is named "In the City for Good"; but some rural people hear these words as "Out of the Country Forever."
- *Straight white men* who are told that "the old givens of white, male, Western, colonial advantage no longer hold."[9] If not those exact words, they have heard other words that tell

them they've got it all wrong and all the problems are their fault.

- *Lifelong church members* who feel that the call to be more "inclusive" doesn't include them. In fact, they feel they are being told to get out of the way to make room for others.
- *Wealthy people* who never hear a good word about people who have money, *homemakers* who feel chastised like Martha, and *married people* who feel that marriage is being discounted. You can add people you know to the list. Perhaps you would add your own name.

"I tell you, God is able from these stones to raise up children to Abraham." John's words remain both a wondrous and frightening promise. One of the biggest challenges to the preacher is to help people envision a table that includes those we never thought to ask to dinner. It also means that some sermons each year should intentionally reach out to the elder brother or sister who can't yet join in the dancing. This doesn't mean watering down Jesus' passion for the outcasts, prostitutes, and tax collectors. It doesn't mean rescinding the invitation to poor people, crippled people, lame people, and blind people (Luke 14:13, 23). It *does* mean paying attention to those who feel they've been left behind. The preacher steps into the pulpit with the astonishment of the servant sent into the streets and lanes of the town by his master to fill the seats at the wedding banquet: "Sir, what you have ordered has been done, and there is still room" (Luke 14:22). Nobody has to leave. Just set another place at the table.

SERMON: A STRANGE BEGETTING

Luke 3:7-18 (Advent)

*"For I tell you, God is able from these stones to raise up children to Abraham." (Luke 3:8*b*)*

Before Pokemon, before Cabbage Patch dolls or Tickle-Me Elmo, before Nintendo or skate boards, there were Pet Rocks. Do you remember? They were ordinary rocks sold in a carrying case shaped like a little house. I can't remember if the rocks came with names or if you named your own.

A young man I once knew—let's call him Harold—had a pet rock before anybody thought of selling them. He got his for nothing before pet rocks were even invented. It must have been thirty years ago when I first met Harold. I was a youth director at a church in the Midwest. Harold wasn't one of "our kids"; that is, he wasn't part of our congregation, or any congregation. He didn't live in our neighborhood, and I can't remember whether he found us or we found him.

I do remember that Harold was a chubby guy for a sixth grader. He lived with his mother in a falling-down apartment about a mile from the church. There was no father around, but there were lots of men. That's what Harold told us, at any rate. Harold found us sometime before summer, and I convinced him to go with us to camp. It certainly wasn't his idea. Though things weren't terrific at home, at least he knew home. But he had never even been outside the city limits.

Harold wasn't accustomed to doing the kinds of projects other campers had come to expect. One afternoon we asked everyone to make collages—it was, after all, the late sixties, the "Era of Collages." There were piles of magazines and newspapers all over the floor. The campers tore into them, searching for pictures or words that would say something about themselves. They had done this before. Harold was finished before anyone else. The others kept tearing and pasting until their pages were filled with images. Harold's page had only one picture: a road sign that said WRONG WAY. When we went around the circle, Harold didn't want to talk about it.

It was at camp that Harold found his rock. He didn't know anybody well and the rock became his closest companion. It sat by him at mealtime while everybody else was singing songs about getting your elbows off the table and other stupid songs Harold didn't know. When everyone joined in singing around the fireplace at night, Harold sat as silent as his stone.

The other kids didn't know quite what to make of Harold. He didn't go to school with any of them, and he was, well, different. It was clear, though, that Harold was fond of his rock. Here was a friend who never failed him, never sassed or hit or bullied him, and never laughed at his size or asked about his family. He never had to worry about being picked last for the softball team because he could count on his rock to sit on the bench beside him.

Slowly, Harold and his rock entered the life of the camp. The other kids started saying "hello" to his rock, and sometimes they even got through to Harold. Before long, Harold was translating what his rock was trying to say, and soon it sounded like a real conversation. One night, he even began to sing, until he realized someone was looking. When the bus came at the end of the week, Harold and his rock refused to get on. He begged and begged to stay. He said that he could help the younger kids who had just arrived—after all, he was big for his age. We said, "Okay, one more week." Who could turn down a boy and his rock? Harold introduced his rock to all the little kids. He even told them his own name: "I'm Harold," he said, and for the first time, it didn't sound like an apology.

"I tell you," said John [the Baptist], "God is able from these stones to raise up children to Abraham." I would add Sarah, too, though John forgot. I know—John wasn't talking about Harold's rock. But he could have been talking about Harold. Or anybody who feels they could never be called a "child of God." There's a lot in this Gospel text—judgment, a call to genuine repentance, and warnings to those who trust ancestry and bloodline as proof of God's favor—but there will be another time to speak about all of these things. Right now I want *you* to know that God is able to do what we cannot do: God is able, from these stones, to raise up children to Abraham and Sarah. God can beget chosen people where the unchosen stand.

God can do this begetting anywhere at any time—not just at summer camp. I've invited a poet to help us visit some other places where God is raising up children from stones. The poet's name is Gerhard Frost. He's gone now, but his poems in *Seasons of a Lifetime* lift up God's presence in every age of our lives, from the spring of childhood to the winter of old age. I'll begin with a poem set in winter.

> Riverplace
> they call it,
> the new shopping mall,
> resplendent, teeming,
> all dressed up
> for Christmas.
>
> My feet are tired
> but I don't go home.
> I find a bench, a place
> beside a solitary man.
> I sense there's something,
> I feel it, something
> he has a need to tell.

Immediately, but shyly,
tentatively, he says:
"My wife died just
two months ago."[10]

Remember, friend, *remember the Christmas child.* If you feel too much loss and loneliness, remember that Jesus wept at the death of his dear friend Lazarus and felt completely abandoned on the cross. The poet wrote this poem in the waning years of his own life. If you feel too old to receive the promises of God, remember Simeon and Anna. They were well on in years, yet they were among the first to hold the child Jesus. "My own eyes have seen God's salvation," Simeon sang. God is not bound by the required age for retirement. God is able, from the stone of isolation and loneliness, to raise up children of promise. God can beget children at any age.

You may not be old or lonely today, but you may feel tradition's stones weighing on you, shutting you out of God's family. Maybe you are gay or lesbian; maybe your child is. Someone somewhere told you there's no place for you or for your son or daughter among God's chosen people. Someone told you that you must be someone other than who you are to come to the table. Listen, my friend. The poet has a word to surprise you, and a word to transform the people who have rejected you:

When your options are either
to revise your beliefs
or to reject a person,
look again.

Any formula for living
that is too cramped
for the human situation
cries for re-thinking.

Hard-cover catechisms
are a contradiction
to our loose-leaf lives.[11]

Remember, friend, *the child Jesus grew up*, and he spent his ministry bumping up against tradition. Jesus healed on the Sabbath and broke down restrictions on God's mercy. When confronted with the choice between healing a person or obeying the rules, Jesus chose the person every time. I tell you, God is able, from the stones of tradition, to raise up children of promise, loved and embraced into fullness of life.

But you may *like* being a stone. "He's a real rock," they say of you, and that can be a good thing indeed. You're steady and strong. You don't need to ask for directions; you'll find the place if it takes all day! You believe what you believe. Or you refuse to believe. And you will never change. The poet has a word for you also:

> Today I learned a lesson,
> the simplest kind of lesson—
> from a fruit jar cover.
>
> My first turn was wrong;
> but I was stubborn,
> and I was strong.
>
> The second was more wrong
> because I was strong.
>
> And now it sticks.
>
> How sad to be strong
> (and stubborn)
> when you're wrong![12]

Remember, friend, *remember the Christmas child, the one named Jesus.* He named one of his disciples Peter, the rock. Peter was strong and sometimes stubborn and sure, but Peter was surprised at every turn. Changed and chastised, Peter had to discover who Jesus was again and again. Peter's assumptions wouldn't do. His strong confessions were confused. But Peter came to see that a rock, too, can be changed. I tell you, God is able to awaken the most stubborn stone, to bring about surprise, to turn "no" into "yes." You may lose your grip, but you will find your life.

The poet may have missed you completely. The preacher may have, too. You can add your own story here at the end, the story you know better than anyone else. There are days when you turn to stone and nothing can touch you, no one can reach you. Bring all of that—bring all that is inside to God. Shout it out, cry and rage, or sit silent as a stone. For the prophet still comes to you, preparing the way of the Lord. John still cries out to awaken you and me to God's life-changing, disruptive power.

"I tell you, God is able from these stones to raise up children to Abraham." It makes for a strange and unpredictable family tree! It surely is a strange begetting. One summer long ago it happened when a boy named Harold was begotten anew as a child of God, and he said his own name without apology.

It's a strange begetting—but thank God it happens again and again. Even this very day. Even to you.

SERMON: BAD FARMING

Matthew 13:24-30, 36-43

*" 'Then do you want us to go and gather [the weeds]?' they asked him. But he replied, 'No; for in gathering the weeds you would uproot the wheat along with them. Let both of them grow together until the harvest.' " (Matthew 13:28*b*-30)*

It's already the middle of the summer, and if I were back on the farm where I grew up, I'd probably be "walking the beans" for the second or third time. Now that phrase may sound odd to you if you've never lived on a farm. Walking the beans is not like walking the dog because, of course, beans don't walk. I walked, and my dad walked—my mom, my sister, and my brother, too. We walked up and down between the mile-long rows of soybeans. Down one row, back up another. We walked acres and acres of soybeans to pull or chop the weeds out of the row. These were the weeds you couldn't get with the cultivator and tractor, weeds right in the midst of the bean plants.

Spotting corn was easy: it grew from seeds dropped in the field the year before. In the cornfield, corn was considered part of the crop, but in the bean field, corn was a weed and had to be chopped out with a machete knife. Sunflowers were easy, too—even before their flowers came out. Thistles were prickly, but not hard to spot. It was the milkweeds that gave me trouble. I knew them after I pulled them because the sticky milk in the stem stuck to my hands and glued my fingers together. But the leaves looked a lot like the leaves of the soybean plants, hiding among the beans to fool people intent on rooting them up. Sometimes, when the day was very hot (which it almost always was in Iowa in July) or when I was very tired and didn't want to be there (which was almost always true), I would get a little careless. I'd start going too fast and get reckless in my pulling. When I looked down at the weed in my hand, it was a beautiful green soybean plant. With luck, my dad would be several rows away from me, and I'd stick the plant back, hoping no one would be around to see it wither and die.

I wish I had been more familiar with Matthew 13 then. I could have told my dad, "Remember what the scripture says, Daddy. Don't pull those weeds; if we gather the weeds, we might uproot the plants along with them. Let them grow together until the harvest." Of course, that would be very bad farming. I don't think my dad would have been convinced. He often coaxed us children into the fields with dire warnings about the farm manager driving by on the county road and seeing our bean fields choked with weeds. We knew that meant we'd be kicked off the farm—for we didn't own the place—and who knows where we would have ended up? After all, one weed wouldn't hurt the bean crop, but thousands of weeds could take over a field. If you let them grow until the harvest there'd be precious little harvest at all.

Why does Jesus keep telling stories about bad farming? Last week, he talked about a sower who scattered seed seemingly at random: on rocky ground and on well-traveled pathways—even in the midst of thistles. Some fell on good soil, but it seemed almost like an accident. My father would never have done that. It was a waste of good seed. Now when I read parables like this, I usually say to myself, "Isn't it wonderful how Jesus used such down-to-earth stories and images? Sowers and sheep, bread dough and fishing nets—these images would certainly make sense to the people of Galilee. Of course people in New York City might be confused, but if Jesus were talking to New Yorkers, he'd find a way to get through."

Then one day it struck me: these parables about sowing seeds and leaving weeds must have sounded completely ridiculous to people who *knew* about farming. Come to think of it, would one shepherd really leave ninety-nine sheep in jeopardy to go searching for one who got lost? Jesus' parables, which seem so simple and clear, don't really make sense at all—not to people who make their living by farming or tending sheep! Did Jesus really mean to draw such pictures of the kingdom of God? Or was he simply a bad farmer?

The seed parables in this thirteenth chapter are crucially important in Matthew's Gospel. This chapter comes right in the middle of the book and is packed with pictures of the kingdom of God. Now, in the first seed parable—the one in which the farmer flings out the seed every which way—Jesus explained to his disciples that the seed was the word of God. But in the second parable, the meaning of the seed has shifted. Jesus says, "The one who sows the good seed is the Son of Man; the field is the world, and the good seed are the children of the kingdom" (Matt. 13:38). In this parable, the good seeds are people: they are children of God's kingdom. And the weeds sown by the evil one? They're people, too. Jesus tells us that the good seeds and the bad weeds will grow up together, side by side, until the harvest. And we're not supposed to pull or chop or spray the weeds lest we destroy the good along with the bad.

This is bad farming. And it's no way to run a kingdom. Jesus' disciples probably didn't like the parable any better than we do. What good is it to be in the kingdom of God if we're surrounded by bad seed? Well, this was a problem. So it didn't take long for people who thought they knew more than Jesus to redefine the kingdom. The disciples themselves had a hard time with Jesus' vision. Some of them argued about who would be greatest; they protested when people who weren't part of their group cast out demons. Jesus didn't seem concerned about the competition. He kept talking about the first being last and the last first. They began to wonder what sort of kingdom this was.

It wasn't easy for the disciples to live the vision of Jesus' kingdom. There were constant temptations to pull up the weeds that seemed to be growing up all around them. The earliest churches also had weeding problems. Arguments broke out about who was in and who was out. There were questions about eating certain foods, disagreements about speaking in tongues, and pronouncements about who should remain silent in worship. Rules were established to determine who belonged to the kingdom of God and who did not.

It has been very hard for the church to wait for God's harvest. Over the centuries since Jesus' resurrection and ascension, the church has often focused more on weeding than planting or tending the garden. If we look at the past two thousand years, we can see that the most tragic eras in the church's life have been caused by this passion for weeding. Crusades were organized to drive infidels from Jerusalem; inquisitions rooted out heretics. Women accused of being witches were thrown into the fire like weeds to be burned. Those who were deemed bad seed were excommunicated and cast out of the church into utter darkness. Structures had to be set up to decide who the weeds were. But the weeds were always people, and sometimes they were judged to be weeds simply because they were different from the groups in power.

What had happened to Jesus' parable? Didn't anybody remember what Jesus said about letting the weeds grow up alongside the good seed? It was just too hard. There was the very real fear that the weeds would overwhelm the good plants altogether. In every generation there are people who think something has to be done to clean up the field.

God, however, is not an all-seeing farm manager driving by to see how many weeds have grown up. Indeed, God may be far more concerned about the weeds we pull up than the weeds we pass by—for the weeds are always people, people who are pointed at, chastised, condemned, cast out. "But Jesus didn't understand how bad it could get in this earthly field!" we protest. "Jesus never met the people we've seen. Besides, aren't Christians supposed to condemn evil? Surely God doesn't want us to let anything go. Can't God see that too many weeds could indeed choke the harvest?"

Jesus' parable wasn't simple when he told it long ago, and it's not simple now. There's a perplexing line about

Jesus in the Apostles' Creed. It comes after "He suffered, died and was buried" and before "And on the third day he rose from the dead." It says, "He descended into hell." (In some translations it says, "He descended to the dead.") If you say this creed, that line may be one you skip over quickly. If you've just heard the words for the first time, that line may seem absurd. Why would Jesus go to hell? Perhaps to preach the gospel of repentance and salvation to those who are there. Jesus was always going where he wasn't supposed to go on earth—why would it be any different when he died?

If Jesus is willing to go to the depths of hell, maybe I can learn to live with a few weeds. Who knows? Somebody else may think that I should be pulled up and thrown away! All I know for certain is this: Jesus told us to stop weeding. It's bad farming, but it's the kingdom of God. If we took Jesus' words to heart, it might change the church more than anything in the past two thousand years has.

CHAPTER THREE

Testing What Is Written in Stone

Joshua's stones are important. They stand as testimony to the children's children long after sea and Sinai are out of view. Rosemary Radford Ruether reminds us of the importance of such stones when she writes about church polity or structure: "The only legitimate discussion of church polity concerns not apostolic polity, but whether polity is capable of both assuring the responsible transmission of the tradition and, at the same time, of being open to new movements of the Spirit by which the meaning of the tradition can come alive."[1] We must bring the stones from the river to help us remember to pass down the story. When the children ask, "What do these stones mean?" someone needs to be able to give them an answer. But we must be more than stonekeepers. Ruether insists that the church also needs "to be open to new movements of the Spirit by which the meaning of tradition can come alive." Stones are not enough. Sometimes stones can be too much, blocking out the winds of God's Spirit. "The optimal polity is the polity that can be most responsible in transmitting and communicating Christian culture while erecting fewest barriers to the workings of the Spirit."[2]

What stones should be remembered as essential to the ongoing life of the faith community? What stones are blocking the Spirit's renewing power? When do stones become downright dangerous? These questions are not easy to answer. Some people see scripture itself as a stone—or a monument of stones—that must not be questioned in any way. Others argue that we must tear down some of scripture's stones in order to be faithful in this generation. After all, didn't Jesus warn us about trusting tradition's stones?

> As [Jesus] came out of the temple, one of his disciples said to him, "Look, Teacher, what large stones and what large buildings!" Then Jesus asked him, "Do you see these great buildings? Not one stone will be left here upon another; all will be thrown down." (Mark 13:1-2)

But tearing down stones can leave nothing but a pile of rubble. Picking away at scripture's stones one by one or in massive exegetical excavations can rob people of a book that has been life giving to them. What has been gained by telling people that the present-day Red Sea was not the biblical Red Sea, that mud clogged the chariot wheels and doomed the Egyptian army while the Hebrew people made it across the sea on foot? (In other words, there's no saving miracle here, no need for God.) Has it transformed people to know Moses didn't write the Pentateuch, that Jonah probably wasn't an historical figure, that Isaiah was written by at least three different writers, or that the nativity stories are creative works of the imagination?

Transformational preaching calls for a "third way," a way between worshiping the stones and throwing them away.[3] Preachers honor the stones set up over centuries, but they also test these stones in the present generation. Jesus gives us the model for this holy work in the Gospel of Matthew. After a series of parables portraying the kingdom of heaven, Jesus turned to his disciples, saying:

> "Have you understood all this?" They answered, "Yes." And [Jesus] said to them, "Therefore every

> scribe who has been trained for the kingdom of heaven is like the master of a household who brings out of his treasure what is new and what is old." (Matt. 13:51-52)

Then Jesus left and went to his hometown, returning to people who had known him and his family for years. He taught in their synagogue—no doubt teaching in the model of the faithful scribe. Those who heard Jesus' teaching took offense at the hometown boy now grown. In Luke's Gospel, the offense becomes deadly:

> [Jesus said,] "Yet today, tomorrow, and the next day I must be on my way, because it is impossible for a prophet to be killed outside of Jerusalem. Jerusalem, Jerusalem, the city that kills the prophets and stones those who are sent to it! How often have I desired to gather your children together as a hen gathers her brood under her wings, and you were not willing!" (Luke 13:33-34)

The stones of remembrance can turn violent. The stones set up to pass on the story can begin to replace God as the focus of worship. In every generation believers are called not only to remember the stones, but also to be open to the wind of the Spirit calling the stones to life. How can we faithfully test the stones of scripture and tradition? How can preachers follow Jesus' model for doing theology as "scribes trained for the kingdom of heaven"?

Jesus' Model for Testing the Stones

Jesus did not leave us helpless and alone in testing the stones. His own teaching provided clues for faithful discernment in each generation. The two intertwined commandments to love God and neighbor stand at the center of the Torah, and Jesus confirmed them as a summary of the whole law:

> "Teacher, which commandment in the law is the greatest?" [Jesus] said to him, " 'You shall love the Lord your God with all your heart, and with all your soul, and with all your mind.' This is the greatest and first commandment. And a second is like it: 'You shall love your neighbor as yourself.' On these two commandments hang all the law and the prophets." (Matt. 22:36-40)

Given the centrality of this double love commandment, what questions might preachers ask to test the stones of scripture and tradition?

Can enslaving another human being ever be consistent with God's command to love our neighbor as ourselves? The tragic history of slavery in the United States must be remembered not only in the historic black churches, but also in every congregation in this country. These stories have shaped our religious heritage as Americans; these stones mark a terrible past "over a way that with tears has been watered."[4]

Womanist theologian Delores Williams tells the story of her grandmother's conversation with her great-grandmother, who had been a slave. "Mama," her grandmother asked, "how can you have the same religion as the white masters?" Without hesitation, her great-grandmother replied, "Child, them and us both Christian, but we ain't got the same religion."[5] Williams's great-grandmother had tested the teachings of white Christianity and found them to be in direct opposition to God's command to love your neighbor as yourself, yet the literal words of the Bible often supported slavery: "One hundred and fifty years ago, when the debate over slavery was raging, the Bible seemed to be clearly on the slaveholders' side. Abolitionists were hard-pressed to justify their opposition to slavery on biblical grounds."[6] The biblical stones that supported slavery had to be blown down by winds of the Spirit to make way for a new exodus.

A related question grows out of the love commandment but is more pointed in discerning harmful aspects of texts themselves. *Have biblical texts or interpretations harmed human beings, including women?* "Including women" may seem an unnecessary addition to this question; however, feminist scholarship has tested scripture and church teachings and has discovered that women are often missing and maligned. In recent years forgotten stories of women have been reclaimed and texts that demean women have been exposed as dangerous. Such testing isn't done for the sake of change; it's done to be faithful to God's call in every age and for the well-being of God's children on earth. In her book *Feminist Liturgy,* Janet Walton responds to those who fear that change means only losing:

> Fear of losing what is familiar is a warranted concern. . . . Change is inevitable. But, it does not mean eliminating all that is familiar, all well-loved language for God, all scripture texts, all typical forms of preaching. . . . It does require examining them and giving up whatever hurts, hides, or dishonors.[7]

Testing the stones of scripture and tradition, the faithful scribe challenges whatever "hurts, hides, or dishonors" human beings—including women. Texts that demand women's submission to men have proved dangerous to women's wholeness and well-being. Jesus' words about bearing the cross have been distorted to trap women in destructive, even deadly, relationships.[8]

Phyllis Trible's attentiveness to "texts of terror" has awakened preachers to respond to stories of women misused and abused in the Bible—Hagar, Tamar, Jephthah's daughter, and the Levite's concubine. The anguish of these women was never addressed within scripture or throughout centuries of church tradition. Like the concubine treated so brutally in the book of Judges, a woman sitting in the sanctuary may be waiting for someone to "speak to her heart."[9]

For Christians, Jesus' life and ministry provide critical tests for judging the stones of tradition: hatred and revenge are transformed into loving and praying for enemies (Matt. 5:43-47); wealth cannot be claimed as a sign of God's favor nor poverty as a sign of God's curse (Luke 16:19-31); servanthood, not lording it over others, is the mark of true discipleship (Mark 10:41-45); the foolishness of the cross is greater than human wisdom (1 Cor. 1:18-25). For Christian believers, texts and tradition are tested through the lens of Jesus' life, death, and resurrection.

It is far beyond the scope of this chapter to pose every question that might be useful in testing the stones of traditions and texts. Moreover, it's essential to remember that innovation and change aren't faithful simply because they haven't had time to harden into stone! It's possible for new ideas to be as harmful and demeaning as ancient teachings. Christopher Morse offers the following broad questions for testing both old and new in his book *Not Every Spirit: A Dogmatics of Christian Disbelief*:

> With the biblical witness as confirmed in the ongoing community of faith providing the orientation for their theological task of testing, Christian churches ask specific questions in seeking to recognize when faithfulness requires that some spirit of the times be disbelieved. Is the claim being made continuous with what is apostolic in the tradition? Is it congruent with what the Word of God in scripture is speaking? Is it consistent with the community's prayer and worship? Is it truly catholic, that is, true for the church everywhere and not just in one place? Is it consonant with experience; that is, does it ring true to life in faith? Is it in keeping with a good conscience? What are the effects or consequences? Is the spirit that is being

> advocated pertinent to, or an evasion of, what is crucial, what matters most, in the situation at hand? Is it coherent in relation to contemporary modes of thought? How comprehensive is the particular teaching with respect to the full range of Christian confession?[10]

Bringing What Is "New" Can Be Both Transforming and Threatening

Jesus compares the faithful scribe to a householder who brings out of his treasure not only what is old but also what is new (Matt. 13:51-52). Joseph Sittler speaks of theology having this same dynamic quality: "By *theology* we mean not only a having but a doing—not only an accumulated tradition, but a present task which must be done on the playing field of each generation in actual life. One *has* a theology, to a greater or lesser extent, in order to *do* theology, in order to exercise, administer, manifest this always forward movement."[11]

We do not need to look any farther than scripture to see the people of God *doing* theology. The writings of prophets that are shaped by the Babylonian exile are different from earlier writings before the temple was destroyed. Traditions prohibiting Jews and Gentiles from eating together are overturned in the book of Acts. Paul's eschatology shifts from 1 Thessalonians to Romans. Women are told to keep silence in some of the Epistles yet clearly hold positions of leadership in many of the young churches.

This work of *doing* theology continued after the Christian canon was closed, shaped by the stories that were passed down and by new dilemmas and controversies the Bible didn't directly address. The creeds of the fourth century spoke to particular theological issues of their time, as did the confessional statements of the 1500s. The doctrine of two kingdoms in Lutheran theology has been reshaped by the tragedy of the Holocaust in Germany. No longer should Christians yield unquestioned allegiance to the state, as Romans 13 seems to command.

But new ways of doing theology are not always welcomed. This was true when Jesus returned to his hometown, bringing out of the household of faith what was new and what was old. The hometown people took offense at what Jesus said in Nazareth. At other places along the way, religious leaders charged him with blasphemy. Theologian Elizabeth Johnson describes such reactions as "a hardening of the mind":

> It is not uncommon for those whose certitudes and securities may be threatened by women's emerging theological speech to relegate it to the periphery of importance. Such a hardening of the mind against unwanted wisdom can be called a scotosis. . . . Scotosis results when the intellectual censorship function, which usually operates in a good and constructive manner to select elements to give us insight, goes awry. In aberrant fashion this censorship function works to repress new questions in order to prevent the emergence of unwanted insight. . . . The only remedy is conversion.[12]

This "scotosis" is akin to what scripture calls "hardening the heart." This hardness or refusal to hear is often a response to words of renewal and the call to repentance—whether it is Jeremiah's words condemning empty worship or Luther's preaching salvation by grace rather than works. Scotosis sets in, shoring up tradition's stones and building walls to protect those in authority, but Jesus called his followers to be scribes trained for the kingdom of heaven. Preaching needs to remind people that *both* old and new are needed for the ongoing task of doing theology.

Bringing What Is "New" Moves Beyond the Resources of Scripture and Tradition

Some faith communities, affirming the quadrilateral of scripture, tradition, reason, and experience, may be quite open to receiving wisdom from sources outside the Bible. Yet even the Reformation cry of *sola scriptura* didn't mean rejecting everything else. Lutheran New Testament scholar Arland Hultgren reminds us that "scripture alone" didn't rule out other sources of wisdom:

> It should be recalled that the Reformation principle of *sola scriptura* (Scripture alone), articulated by Luther at the Leipzig Debate in 1519 was to assert the authority of Scripture over against ecclesiastical authorities (such as popes and councils) as a basis for teaching. It was not intended to exclude reason and other sources from our theological, ethical, and social reflection, as though Scripture is our one and only source.[13]

When Dr. Sittler urged us to see theology as "a present task which must be done on the playing field of each generation in actual life," he pointed us toward the need to hear new voices as well as old.[14]

Some of these new voices will come from outside the words of scripture and tradition, and they will be as revolutionary as the discovery that the earth revolves around the sun. Preachers can help people receive new voices as part of God's ongoing revelation just as Jesus promised in John's Gospel: "I still have many things to say to you, but you cannot bear them now. When the Spirit of truth comes, [the Spirit] will guide you into all the truth" (John 16:12-13*a*). It remains true that we must "test the spirits" in each generation, but this is the case with what is old as well as what is new. Many of the most pressing dilemmas cannot be resolved by scripture or tradition alone: nuclear weapons, global warming, *in* *vitro* fertilization, heart and liver transplants, affirmative action, Internet access, and so on.

But, as Arland Hultgren reminds us:

> That does not mean for a moment that the Bible is irrelevant. The Bible awakens us to the need of the neighbor, and of the public good. But it does not by itself prescribe specific solutions. The Bible tells us we should not let people go hungry (Matthew 25:35), for example; but we use human reason to decide whether food stamps, subsidized school lunch, or some other approach makes the most sense. When Jesus sent out his disciples, he told them to be "wise as serpents and innocent as doves" (Matthew 10:16). That is good advice for us, too.[15]

Bringing What Is "New" Doesn't Mean Abandoning the "Old"

Transformational preaching is more than demythologizing and deconstructing. Testing what is written in stone doesn't mean the erosion of all we have received from the past. The preacher comes not to destroy but to discern the Spirit's direction for this time and place. Some will hear every question as an attack on what is old and familiar. We must be intentional in lifting up Jesus' promise that the Spirit will guide us into all the truth (John 16:13) and equally intentional in assuring people that we honor and care for them. People who feel attacked and diminished are seldom open to hearing what is new. Elizabeth Johnson presents a model of such intentionality in her book *She Who Is: The Mystery of God in Feminist Theological Discourse.* Though she warns us about the dangers of scotosis—the hardening of the mind—she plumbs the depths of scripture and tradition for their wisdom. She honors the experience of women and asks hard questions of the church fathers, yet within the same pages, she lifts up the insights of Augustine and Aquinas with genuine gratitude. She works as a faithful scribe, bringing old and new from the household of faith in order to "braid a footbridge between the ledges of classical and feminist Christian wisdom."[16]

This respectful, creative braiding of old and new is far different from judging the tradition as empty or completely oppressive. If people suspect that everything is unraveling, resistance will only increase. Jesus calls us to bring both old and new from the treasury of faith. The stones beside the river still stand guard against amnesia. What do these stones mean? What stories can we pass on to our children? How can the preacher be intentional about honoring the old while being open to new wisdom?

- When challenging an oppressive text, such as the silencing of women in the later Epistles, lift up other stories in the Bible, such as Jesus honoring women as students and evangelists.
- When a sermon upsets a traditional interpretation, take care to plan the liturgy with words and songs that are familiar to assure people that not everything has changed. This is not the day to sing three new hymns and introduce a new liturgical setting.
- If the sermon threatens to leave people asking, "Then what's left in the Bible?" be intentional in naming and claiming the stones that are still being carried from the river. Such remembrance might move beyond the sermon to include congregational response in song or litany of praise:

"In the beginning God created the heavens and the earth."

Praise God from whom all blessings flow.

"I have heard the cry of my people in Egypt and will come to deliver them."

Praise God who sets us free from oppression.

"Hear, O Israel: The Lord is our God, the Lord alone. You shall love the Lord your God with all your heart and with all your soul and with all your might."

Praise God whose word is set upon our doorposts and our gates.

"Those who wait for the Lord shall renew their strength.... They shall run and not be weary, they shall walk and not faint."

Praise God who carries us when we cannot go on.

"Behold, the time is fulfilled, and the kingdom of God has come near; repent, and believe in the good news."

Praise God who calls us again and again to repentance and faith.

"I will not leave you orphaned," said Jesus. "The Holy Spirit whom the Father will send in my name will teach you everything."

Praise God who sends the Spirit to guide and renew every generation.

"Now faith is the assurance of things hoped for, the conviction of things not seen."

Praise God who gives us hope beyond our understanding.

"The commandment we have from God is this: those who love God must love their brothers and sisters also."

Praise God whose deep love transforms us from strangers into friends.

"Then I saw a new heaven and a new earth;...and I heard a loud voice from the throne saying, 'See, the home of God is among mortals.'"

Praise God who was, who is, and who will be forever. Amen.

(Adapted from Gen. 1:1; Exod. 3:7; Deut. 6:4-5; Isa. 40:31; Mark 1:15; John 14:18, 26*a*; Heb. 11:1; 1 John 4:21; and Rev. 21:1*a* and 3*a*.)

Once more God's people gather at the river, touching the stones and rehearsing the story. Some of the stones have been washed and reshaped by the water. Others have been thrown down or completely transformed. Some have come to life. Praise God from whom all blessings flow.

SERMON: GOD'S WORD ON THE DOORPOST

Deuteronomy 6:4-9

"And these words which I command you today shall be in your heart; you shall teach them diligently to your children.... You shall write them on the doorposts of your house and on your gates." (Deut. 6:6-9 NKJV)

Every Wednesday afternoon at 2:30 they gather around the table: six Jewish women—all of them over sixty. The table is surrounded by gray hair. They have come not to clean the kitchen or to embroider names on the seder tablecloth, though they have done these things many times. On Wednesdays they come to learn Hebrew. They come because the rabbi, herself a woman, remembers when she was a child, when girls were not taught Hebrew alongside the boys. So now, in their sixties, these women cannot read the Torah in the Sabbath service. They must trust phonetic spelling on the page—words they have learned to pronounce but not fully understand. Slowly, they read around the circle, saying the ancient letters aloud, writing the words on paper, right to left, always right to left. On Wednesday afternoon at 2:30 six women are learning to touch the word as they have never done before.

Why would these women do such a thing after all those years of Sabbath services, years of Passover seders and candle blessings—without knowing a word of Hebrew? Why now? I can't speak for these women, though I have come to know them well over the years. We share a common worship space—Lutherans and Reform Jews. We also share the kitchen, each cupboard carefully labeled. On Wednesdays they invite me for lunch before their study begins. My guess is that something inside these women longed to read the words for themselves. Age did not matter. They had been invited to write the word on the doorposts of their lives.

There must have been some of that same excitement when Martin Luther first translated the Bible into German, the language of the people. Even though few could read any language for themselves, hearing the words of scripture in the language of daily life—the parables in words used at the table or in the marketplace, or the Christmas story in words a mother or father would use to speak about the birth of their own child—was radically new. So simple a thing, yet so different. So much closer to the life of each person. Such translations are human words that draw men, women, and children deeper into the heart of God. To touch the word in this way is an ordinary event on the edge of revelation.

Perhaps you remember a movie called *The Miracle Worker*, which told the story of Helen Keller's struggle to break through her silent world. Born both blind and deaf, she could neither learn sign language nor read lips; she couldn't hear someone describe a color, a tree, or a face. She was locked inside herself, her other senses taking in textures and smells but never sight or sound. Her teacher, Anne Sullivan, worked with her day after day, patiently enduring Helen's outbursts of anger and frustration. Then one afternoon, in the movie, the two of them are at the water pump. Helen feels the water pouring into her hands; her teacher taps into her palm the sign for water. The water flowing. The word tapped from hand to hand. The water. The word. Water. Word. And suddenly, Helen's face comes to life. The water connects with the word. That sign, that tapping—it means this wet-flowing-cold in my hand. She repeats the tapping for herself—a connection, one hand to the other. Water to word. In the middle of a summer afternoon, a girl locked inside her silent, sightless world touched the word. She could hear it and speak it to another human being. It isn't necessary to say that it changed everything.

On a Wednesday afternoon six older women are learning Hebrew—and long ago on a Sunday morning, German farmers, carpenters, homemakers, and children heard a parable in words they used around the table. The words were tapped into their hands and their heads: water/word/water/word. And they knew the two were connected.

The connection changes everything. Sometimes obviously, but other times internally, under the skin, inside the mind and heart. Either way, the connection is always important, never insignificant. The connection between word and self is a connection that is always larger than one self—it changes the connection between Helen and her teacher, between one human being and another. I hear you speaking to me! Surely that was part of the miracle of Pentecost celebrated last Sunday: I am from another country, but I hear you speaking my language and I understand.

There is another connection, however, that is even bigger when the word that is touched is the word we call "God's word"—scripture, the Bible. When the word that is spoken and heard is liturgy, hymn, or prayer—human words stammering a connection between people and God. These are human words, yet we claim that they have a power different from water in the pump or grocery lists or table talk. We believe that these words help us connect the water and the groceries and the table talk to the one we call *God*. When that connection is made, our lives are changed: we stand on holy ground and see blessings where only groceries had been before. God has touched our lives and named them holy.

Our ancestors in the faith stood in awe before this holy word of God. They sensed its power, its wisdom, but this holy word of God was not to them a word far off. They believed this word was near them. It was a word connected to everything that happens in a day, a lifetime:

> And these words which I command you today shall be in your heart; you shall teach them diligently to your children, and shall talk of them when you sit in your house, when you walk by the way, when you lie down, and when you rise up. You shall bind them as a sign on your hand, and they shall be as frontlets between your eyes. You shall write them on the doorposts of your house and on your gates. (Deut. 6:6-9 NKJV)

What is left out? Nothing. This word is connected to sitting and walking, to lying down and rising up. This word is so close it is bound on our hands and worn between our eyes. We must write it on our gates and on our doorposts to mark our homes, to ensure that we never go out or in without seeing the word of God. On my street I watch the Jewish children running in and out to play, reaching up to touch the *mezzuzah* on the door-frame—touching it quickly, but touching it every time. Touching the words of Deuteronomy tucked inside the tiny metal ark. God's word must be tapped into our hands; it must touch our palms. Water, it says—life, water, blessing, nearness. Not far off, but inside my own door and under my skin.

The gray-haired women sit around the table spelling out the Hebrew words, right to left. Our ancestors—German, Swedish, Mexican, French, Tanzanian, Chinese—heard Jesus' parable in their own languages, and their doorposts would never look the same. This longing to touch God's word is very deep; it is a longing that lasts a lifetime. We long not only to know that there *is* such a thing as "God's word," but also to know we are somehow connected to that word. We want it tapped into our hands. We want to sing hymns with our stories embedded in the verses, to hear ourselves addressed by name. How different it sounds when the church gathers to pray not only "for all the sick" but also for Hannah, John, Christopher, and Elizabeth by name.

This is why we struggle so hard to find the right word, new language that is closer to each person—words that invite everyone into God's holy word, words that make the connection between God's word and the doorpost of *my* house, *your* house. Words that name not mankind but humankind, not only sons but also daughters. Not only Caucasian, but African American and Latino, Asian and Native American. Not only grown-ups but also children. This is not so much an attempt to *change* the word of God as it is to find the fullness of the word, to feel it tapped into our minds and our hearts.

What does it mean when women hear a word not spoken before? "You shall be called sons and daughters of God." Sons *and* daughters. Some will not notice. Others will sense that something is different, like a room rearranged, but will not be sure what exactly has changed. Little by little, the sacred word will be tapped out in everyone's hand: man, woman, child. The connections may not be dramatic—not so immediately life changing as water and word connected in Helen's hand—but it will come to pass: a woman, even one, who has never heard her name, her gender, her experience, or her story will begin to see the connection. God's word with her word. A quiet tapping. An invitation to touch the ancient word, to reach out and touch the hem of Jesus' garment, to feel in her own skin that the Word became flesh.

Such a connection is always larger than one hand or one life. Women who know that men have heard and honored their stories will be open to hearing men in new ways. There will be closer connections and fuller speaking for all people. The search for new images, the awkward stumbling over *he* or *she*, the uneasy laughter and anger over changes—all of these things are the work of *translation.* This work is never easy: sitting at the table like a child when you are sixty, learning to read right to left, always right to left. Finding just the right German word in exchange for the Latin: will it be too simple, too ridiculous? Will people laugh where they should weep? Taking Helen's hand one more time under the water, then tapping out the word. Will she ever get it? Perhaps tomorrow.

Such work is not a passing fancy, nor is it a fad: it is work born of faithfulness and longing. It is embraced because we are people who believe the word of God is near, not far off. This word must be written on *our* doorposts, on *our* gates, on *our* hands, and between *our* eyes. We are tapping out the word of God in each other's hands. Sister: Brother: Woman: Man. We are translati slowly, speaking words we hadn't dared befo Speaking of God who is both Mother and Father to us, God who is gentle, almighty, tender, all-knowing. God's word is living, always pouring into our hands, tapping gently but insistently—water/word/water/word. Until we make the connection between God's word and our own lives, and our doorposts will never be the same.

SERMON:
THE FEAR IN OUR HOMETOWN

Luke 4:21-30

Then [Jesus] began to say to them, "Today this scripture has been fulfilled in your hearing." (Luke 4:21)

We have come into this Gospel text in the middle of the story—like walking in late for a movie. The reel has been running a while, and we'll have to find our place and make sense of the scene. Jesus is speaking. "Today," he says, "this scripture has been fulfilled in your hearing." You may have seen this movie before, so you know what scripture Jesus is talking about. Or perhaps this is all new to you.

Jesus had just read from the scroll of the prophet Isaiah:

> The Spirit of the Lord is upon me,
> because he has anointed me
> to bring good news to the poor.
> He has sent me to proclaim release to the captives
> and recovery of sight to the blind,
> to let the oppressed go free,
> to proclaim the year of the Lord's favor. (Luke 4:18-19)

Then Jesus rolled up the scroll and sat down. The eyes of all in the synagogue were fixed on him. All of this happened before we came in. If this were a movie, the camera would be panning around the room, focusing on faces, eyes wide, bodies bending forward. Or perhaps the camera would focus on Jesus. This is where we came in—as Jesus begins to speak: "'Today this scripture has been fulfilled in your hearing.' [And] all spoke well of him and were amazed at [his] gracious words" (4:21). The voices in the room grow louder. People are talking in groups; the camera moves in, allowing us to overhear. "Is not this Joseph's son?" someone asks. The scene moves quickly. I doubt that any director could manage this scene. It goes too fast. We have no time to take it in.

Jesus speaks again. Already the mood has changed. Jesus senses their uneasiness and suspicion. "Doubtless you will quote to me this proverb, 'Doctor, cure yourself!' And you will say, 'Do here also in your hometown the things that we have heard you did at Capernaum.' " (They hadn't mentioned Capernaum; Jesus seems to be reading their minds.) "No prophet is accepted in the prophet's hometown," he says (4:23-24). What does Jesus see in their eyes? Hear in their questions? By now people must be visibly agitated. *Does this man think he's a prophet?* Then Jesus goes on, reminding them of two stories most of them had heard since childhood.

Two of Israel's prophets, Elijah and Elisha, had healed and blessed outsiders—a widow from Sidon and a leper from Syria—though, as Jesus pointed out, there were surely widows and lepers in Israel at the time. It's hard to follow what he's saying, especially if you don't know the stories. I remember that second story, the leprosy story, from my childhood. In *Egermeier's Bible Story Book* there was a picture of the little Hebrew servant girl who brought her master, Naaman, to Elisha the prophet. Naaman was a powerful Syrian soldier. He wanted to wash in a Syrian river to be made clean, but Elisha was stubborn and insisted that he come to the Jordan. I can still see the picture of the little girl standing beside the prophet and the Syrian soldier. The mighty soldier was dripping wet, and perhaps embarrassed, but the leprosy was gone. I thought it was a great story.

But there's no time to stay with those memories for long. The story in the synagogue has already moved on. We have gone only six verses since Jesus sat down. Only six verses since all spoke so well of him. Suddenly, "all in the synagogue were filled with rage" (4:28). How could things get so bad in six verses? The camera moves over the faces—the same faces that had spoken well of him, faces now red with rage.

> They got up, drove him out of the town, and led him to the brow of the hill on which their town was built, so that they might hurl him off the cliff. (4:29)

Wait! What did Jesus say that was so bad? Have they forgotten? This is Joseph's son. They'd known him all of his life. It's one thing to disagree, but this rage is out of proportion. There's no reason to throw this hometown boy over the cliff. Jesus "passed through the midst of them and went on his way" (4:30).

What had happened in Jesus' hometown? Let's go back to where we entered the scene. "Today this scripture has been fulfilled in your hearing." Was that it? Had Jesus' words sunk in? Was Joseph's son claiming to be the one anointed by the Spirit of God? Or was it the stories he told—the widow in Sidon, the leper in Syria—did he think they wouldn't get the point? Had God moved out of Nazareth—is that what Jesus was saying? It isn't hard to imagine that the people in Nazareth would take offense at him or be a bit put off, but they were filled with rage. They wanted to kill him.

"Today this word has been fulfilled in your hearing." The camera fades out, then back. The scene has changed and so has the time. It's not a synagogue, but Saint George's Church in Philadelphia in 1787. Two black ministers, Richard Allen and Absalom Jones, are pulled from their knees as they pray in a church gallery reserved for whites. There was a place for blacks in the balcony, but they refused to go. Instead, they passed through the midst of them and led their people out into the light of day. *What do these people want?* the white folks must have asked. *We ordained these men to attend to the needs of black people. How many other churches would have done that?* But the two black preachers believed that the fullness of God's blessing had come upon them and their people, and they would acknowledge those blessings by praying on the main floor—if not in this church, then somewhere else. Thus the African Methodist Episcopal Church was born.

"Today this word has been fulfilled in your hearing." The Spirit's anointing does not go unnoticed. Jesus went to Capernaum—and Philadelphia. He even came to my small town and my home church: Zion Lutheran, Gowrie, Iowa. It's a silly story, really. Nothing as memorable as the preachers in Philadelphia, but I guess it was memorable for a child. Every year our Sunday school presented a Christmas pageant. And every year, I was in the chorus: the angel chorus or the speech chorus or some other chorus. But Mary was played by a girl who hardly ever came to Sunday school. My mother tried to explain that it was the teacher's way of getting her involved, but it made no sense to me. After all, I was the one who was always there.

A widow in Sidon. A leper in Syria. Two African American ministers in Philadelphia. The wrong girl chosen to be Mary in an Iowa town. And the people in Nazareth—people like me who are there week in and week out—are supposed to keep singing their hearts out in the chorus. The people in Jesus' hometown heard what Jesus was saying: God has blessed and healed *out-*

siders before, and God is doing it again. And they were filled with rage.

"Today," said Jesus, "this scripture is fulfilled in your hearing." This word *changes* things. This word proclaims good news to the poor and release to the captives. When African American slaves heard Jesus reading from the prophet Isaiah, they must have wondered in their hearts, for they surely didn't hear much good news or experience much freedom. But one day that word came to Richard Allen and Absalom Jones with anointing power. "Today this scripture is fulfilled in your hearing"—*your* hearing, brothers and sisters. And they stood up and led their people across the Jordan River instead of up to the balcony. This word fulfilled changes things.

Those who are lifelong Christians would surely say that God's blessings are meant for everyone. I was taught that lesson in Zion's Sunday school years ago. The white Christians in church that Sunday in Philadelphia no doubt said that God's blessings were for everyone. The people in Jesus' hometown probably did, too. But when this happens on God's terms and not ours, we get a little miffed. Even outraged. Can you hear the voices?

> *Of course we believe that God loves everybody—not just white people. We'd never ask black sisters and brothers to sit in the balcony today! But now they want us to add spirituals to our hymnal and change the pictures in the Sunday school books. We admit the children in the books used to be mostly white—but that changed years ago. Now they're talking about the pictures of Jesus. Don't you think that's going a bit too far?*

It's hard to be from Nazareth these days. Hard to hear the stories about all the outsiders that God is calling and blessing. I guess some of us feel a bit like I did years ago when the wrong girl got to play Mary and I was an anonymous angel singing offstage. Sometimes we joke about how much things have changed, but sometimes we don't. In the Lutheran Church we're not even sure what jokes you can tell anymore. We assume the Scandinavian jokes about Ole and Lena will probably have to go. Maybe the Swedish smorgasbords, too. I don't know how it is in your church, if you're part of one, but there are lots of people in Nazareth who feel like they've been left behind or passed over. To them, everything that matters is happening in Capernaum; everybody who matters lives somewhere else.

How will it be in Nazareth in this new year? In the Lutheran Church in the United States 1995 marked the twenty-fifth anniversary of the ordination of women. There are about 1,700 ordained women out of some 16,000 clergy in our denomination. Nevertheless, it is not uncommon to hear that women are taking over the church. There are too many women on church boards, too many women appointed as delegates to important meetings. Sometimes I hear my brother pastors say, "I'll never be elected to anything again. I'm white, and I'm a man, and the seats are reserved for somebody else."

There's a lot of fear in our hometowns, in our congregations, and in the larger church. A lot of fear and rage in Nazareth. But Jesus won't take back what he said after reading from Isaiah: "Today this scripture has been fulfilled in your hearing." Some will argue that Isaiah's scripture has nothing to do with the two Black preachers in Philadelphia or with women being ordained—Luke's story is about *Jesus* fulfilling the prophecy. Then what do we mean when we pray for the Spirit's power? It happens every time there is a baptism in our church. The words in italics say, *"The minister lays both hands on the head of each of the baptized and prays for the Holy Spirit."*[17] The prayer is not new; the words come from the book of Isaiah. "Pour out your Holy Spirit upon ______: the spirit of wisdom and understanding, the spirit of counsel and might, the spirit of knowledge and the fear of the Lord, the spirit of joy in your presence."[18] These words are from a different chapter of Isaiah than the words Jesus read, but aren't we praying for the *same* Spirit?

"Today this scripture is fulfilled in your hearing." This word fulfilled changes things. In Nazareth and Capernaum. In Philadelphia and in my hometown and in yours, too. The story could have been different in Jesus' hometown. The people could have believed God's word was being fulfilled that very day in their hearing. They could have believed the word was meant for them. But they were thinking about Capernaum—and I was thinking about that undeserving girl who played Mary, and the white people in the church in Philadelphia thought the Black preachers were asking for far too much.

The story in Nazareth didn't have to end with rage. It could have ended with blessing. "Today this word is fulfilled in your hearing." It's the same in your hometown and mine. The promises of God are big enough for you and me—and for the people of Capernaum. Let us pray for a deep measure of the Spirit's anointing so we can trust God's blessing enough to quiet our fear and our rage.

CHAPTER FOUR

Bearing the Hard Words

The Reverend Will B. Dunn, the cartoon preacher created by Doug Marlette, is standing in the pulpit: "Brothers and sisters," he preaches, "We gotta be willin' to give up all this drinkin'!"

"Amen!" shouts the congregation.

". . . and smokin'!"

"Amen!"

"And carryin' on!"

"Amen!"

"Yessir, we gotta be willin' to give up these video cassette recorders!"

Silence. Not a word.

The Reverend's thoughts appear in a bubble: "I think I touched a nerve!"[1]

Hard words aren't so hard if they're about somebody else, but when they get too close, such words are often impossible to hear. It can be tempting to avoid hard words altogether, to seek words of comfort rather than confrontation. Yet confrontation is not the goal. God longs for transformation: transformation of individual human beings *and* the whole creation. Hard words may be needed to break through the solid walls of self-sufficiency and awaken us to God's alternative vision. But hard words are hard to bear.

Hard Words Have a Long History

The people of Israel often had a hard time hearing hard words. The first tablets of stone ended up shattered and broken at the foot of the mountain. The stones lay broken beyond repair. Moses burned the golden calf they had made, ground it into powder, mixed it with water, and made the people drink it. And that was that.

But for God, that wasn't that. Two chapters later God begins all over again.

> The LORD said to Moses, "Cut two tablets of stone like the former ones, and I will write on the tablets the words that were on the former tablets, which you broke. . . ." So Moses cut two tablets of stone like the former ones; and he rose early in the morning and went up on Mount Sinai, as the LORD had commanded him, and took in his hand the two tablets of stone. (Exod. 34:1, 4)

After the people had crossed the Jordan, after the stones were set up at Gilgal, Joshua called the people together at Shechem. Once more God renewed the covenant made with them at Sinai, and once more the people said, "Yes!" But Joshua warned them that it was hard—indeed, it was almost impossible—to keep this covenant, for "[God] is a jealous God." The people insisted, "The LORD our God we will serve." Then Joshua took a large stone, and set it up under the oak in the sanctuary of the Lord. Joshua said to the people, "See, this stone shall be a witness against us; for it has heard all the words of the LORD that he spoke to us" (Josh. 24:19-27*a*).

Once more, a stone. A stone set up as a witness—a stone with ears! The stone set up at Shechem bears witness not only to God's enduring promise, but also to the reality that this covenant is not easy to keep on the human side of the equation.

Jesus Didn't Set the Hard Words Aside

"Do not think that I have come to abolish the law or the prophets; I have come not to abolish but to fulfill" (Matt. 5:17). Jesus spoke these words in the Sermon on the Mount, between a series of unusual blessings and words about keeping the law. Teaching as a scribe trained for the kingdom of heaven, Jesus seems to set some laws aside, or at least change their interpretation dramatically: "You have heard that it was said, 'An eye for an eye and a tooth for a tooth.' But I say to you, Do not resist the evildoer" (Matt. 5:38-39*a*). He also said, "You have heard that it was said, 'You shall love your neighbor and hate your enemy.' But I say to you, Love your enemies and pray for those who persecute you" (Matt. 5:43-44).

On the other hand, when Jesus interprets two of the Ten Commandments, he doesn't argue against them; rather, he deepens and expands their application:

> You have heard that it was said to those of ancient times, "You shall not murder"; and "whoever murders shall be liable to judgment." But I say to you that if you are angry with a brother or sister, you will be liable to judgment; and if you insult a brother or sister, you will be liable to the council; and if you say, "You fool," you will be liable to the hell of fire. (Matt. 5:21-22)

These are hard words! It's tempting to say that Jesus was engaging in exaggeration to get our attention, but he continues with specific guidance about the difficult words he has just spoken: "So when you are offering your gift at the altar, if you remember that your brother or sister has something against you, leave your gift there before the altar and go; first be reconciled to your brother or sister, and then come and offer your gift" (Matt. 5:23-24). Jesus expects his followers to take his words seriously, to observe the law even more deeply than they were accustomed to doing.

He moves on to another commandment: "You shall not commit adultery." Here a command used most often to condemn women is spoken primarily to men: "But I say to you that everyone who looks at a woman with lust has already committed adultery with her in his heart" (Matt. 5:27-28). This word isn't easy either. Jesus holds us accountable for our thoughts even if we don't act on them! Jesus isn't trying to be unreasonably hard-hearted with such interpretations. He is moving us to deepen our understanding of what it means to love God and neighbor, moving us to see God's commonwealth in our midst.

Hard Words Move from Critique to Provocative Alternatives

Jesus sees what others do not yet see. "Jesus' faith in God is constitutionally restless. He has an incurable eschatological itch. He lives from a dream, the kingdom, or world, of God, and he is committed to the discipline of seeing that dream become a fact."[2] Ethicist Larry Rasmussen outlines three aspects of Jesus' power. He says, "Jesus' power is considerably more than these. But I do not think it is less."

- The power of unrelenting critique (or the power to unravel the cocoon of worldview and ideology).
- The power of a catholic vision (or the power to forge inclusive community).
- The power of pioneering creativity (or the power to forge provocative alternatives).[3]

It doesn't take long to realize that such notions of power will run into opposition, not only in first-century Palestine but in twenty-first-century America as well. How can Jesus' vision of God's commonwealth be preached in the midst of radically different definitions of power?

Hard Words: Wealth and Poverty as a Case Study

Biblical words about wealth and poverty are hard to hear. Throughout scripture we find relentless critique of the gap between rich and poor. Even in the Deuteronomic writings, in which wealth seems to be a sign of God's favor, there are clear commands to care for the widow and the orphan. This concern is heightened in the writings of the prophets and is lifted up again and again in the teachings of Jesus. Trusting in wealth prevents us from loving God with heart, mind, and strength; it also hardens hearts and keeps us from loving our neighbors. Jesus' words about possessions are hard words to hear—they were hard for the disciples, who were astounded at his teachings (Mark 10:26), and they are hard for many Christians in the United States. Though we may not count ourselves as rich, most of us are wealthier by far than millions of the world's people. It's a constant temptation for us to temper Jesus' words by pointing to those much wealthier than we are. We pray, "Forgive us our debts as we also have forgiven our debtors," but we turn the word *debts* into a metaphor that never touches economic realities. Sri Lankan theologian Tissa Balasuriya asks a haunting question: "Why is it after millions of eucharistic celebrations, Christians continue as selfish as before?"[4]

How can people hear Jesus' critique of wealth and possessions?

- The preacher stands *with* the people, hearing Jesus' critique of our economic arrangements, our fascination with wealth (both having it and wanting it), and our disregard for the poor among us. The pronoun used in such preaching is always *we* rather than *you*. "Preaching as local theology calls upon pastors to reclaim a renewed sense of 'with-ness'—moving to the pulpit out of the midst of the congregation to give witness to the congregation's own deepest beliefs, doubts, questions, longings, and fears, while also standing with the congregation before a God who confronts and challenges us all."[5]

- The critique can be raised as questions rather than indictments:
  - ➢ Why is it that at the end of 1999, an economic boom year, donations to the New York Times "Neediest Cases Fund" dropped off so dramatically?
  - ➢ Why do we worry more about homeless people ruining the quality of life in our cities than the quality of life for homeless people themselves?
  - ➢ Why is it so easy to name people far richer than ourselves—Internet billionaires and athletic superstars—while we have a hard time acknowledging that most of the world's people are far poorer than any of us?

"But criticism alone is simply cruel; and Jesus said more than the Aramaic equivalent of 'everything is tottering' and 'woe to you scribes, lawyers, Pharisees, and rich ones of this present and passing age.'"[6] Jesus' power also forged inclusive community.

How can preaching help forge inclusive community across the gaps?

Stories can get through where statistics overwhelm. Preaching can open eyes and hearts to those we may not see. The barriers dividing rich people and poor people are often harder to cross than racial divides. Gated communities, private beaches, Internet access, school district lines, and zoning laws keep us from seeing or meeting each other. Freeways now ring many cities, making it possible for people to drive in and out, insulated from neighborhoods they left behind or never knew. In the 1980s the boarded-up windows of apartment buildings in the Bronx were covered with decals so commuters on the expressway would see potted plants and window shades rather than burned-out, gutted interiors. The people who lived in those neighborhoods were too close to the buildings to see the lovely panels high above the street. Like Isaiah or Amos standing in the marketplace, the preacher acts as a seer—not to predict the future but to *see* what's really there and help others see more fully.

- Sermons can take people on a visual tour of the community and let them look at economic realities they may have missed along the way: boarded-up factories, farm foreclosures, high-rise apartments selling for $1.1 million and up, the welfare hotel on the next corner. Heidi Neumark, a pastor in the South Bronx, invites us on a subway ride between two very different neighborhoods:

  > Last week, I went to a meeting of the Nehemiah Housing Trust . . . that oversees the financing of the Nehemiah Housing being built by people of South Bronx . . . for the working poor. . . . [The] meeting took place in the law office of one of their Trust members. . . . This is what I passed in a two block area of 5th Ave. in Manhattan: Fendi, Asprey, Trump Tower, Prada, Tiffany, Bulgari, Mercedes-Benz, Cartier, Mikimoto, Piaget, Merrill Lynch, Steuben, Disney, Reveillon, Christian Dior.
  >
  > At the meeting, those of us from the South Bronx had to justify every cent spent on construction before checks were signed. We did. . . . Then tunneling back to the Bronx, I came out of the subway at Longwood Ave. and passed these stores: Mama's

Fried Chicken, Holy Care Discount, Checks Cashed, Pop's Candy Store, Dinero Express, Alex Wines and Liquors, Mexico Unisex Beauty Salon, Mi Jesus Fruits and Vegetables, Botanica La Caridad . . . and Illusions 99¢ Store.

My guess is that there were not many people gazing into the windows of Tiffany's and Illusions 99¢ Store on the same morning. That's too bad because it does a lot for the renewal of the mind. Will we ever bridge the distance between Mi Jesus Fruits and Vegetables and Cartier? Mercedes-Benz and Pop's Candy Store? Steuben Glass and Diamond Cleaners? Between those who shop there?[7]

- Preaching can present "what if's" to plant seeds that might bring people of different classes together. These ideas should be visionary, but not impossible: the congregation that voted for partnership with a parish in a poorer community rather than building a new addition; a food basket placed in the narthex where some can donate food and others can take the food they need; working with people across classes to build homes through Habitat for Humanity; making sure that church programs and events are not priced beyond the means of the poorest members; and providing child care so parents with young children can participate in these programs without financial hardship.

Forging inclusive community cannot begin until we see each other across the economic divide, and this doesn't happen naturally. A primary challenge for preachers is to be intentional in helping people cross the barriers that separate those who are rich from those who are poor.

How can preaching help people practice provocative alternatives?

Seeing one another across the class divide is itself a provocative alternative that may lead to new ministries and to reassessing priorities. Forging creative partnerships between congregations in poor and wealthy communities can be life-giving for both. But such transformation doesn't happen automatically and it doesn't come naturally. Members of congregations need concrete help to transform personal and public economic patterns. In *Practicing Our Faith: A Way of Life for Searching People,* Dorothy Bass acknowledges the need for down-to-earth "practices" that enable people to live their faith in daily life:

> *Christian practices are things Christian people do together over time in response to and in the light of God's active presence for the life of the world. . . .* When people engage in a practice, they don't just talk about it, though words often play an important part. People-at-practice do things. . . . A Christian community at worship is a community gathered for rehearsal. It is "practicing" the practices in the same way a child practices catching a ball or playing scales. You may not think you need this skill, we tell the child, but stay in the game and the time will probably come when you do.[8]

These words about practicing our faith relate to the third dimension of Jesus' power: forging provocative alternatives. In the story of Jesus' encounter with the rich man, which is found in all three Synoptic Gospels, the rich man always goes away sorrowing, but the narrator makes it clear that Jesus loves this man. Jesus doesn't say, "Sell all you have, give to the poor, then drop me a note to tell me how it's going." Jesus' last words to the man are "Come, follow me." Come and practice in a community of fellow travelers.

It's very difficult to forge provocative alternatives all alone. How can preaching invite people to consider these alternatives in community?

- Advent preaching can help people practice alternative Christmas celebrations within their families and circles of friends and within the congregation.
- The preacher might include a noncanonical lesson one Sunday: "A Reading from My Checkbook on the Eighteenth Sunday After Pentecost" (the appointed Sunday for Mark's story of Jesus and the rich man). The pastor might ask: What do I see as necessary for daily living? What do I call luxuries? Where have I turned "luxuries" into "necessities"?
- Education and information about debt cancellation, socially responsible investments, and micro-lending can be distributed or discussed. The preacher doesn't have to have a degree in economics but can draw upon the wisdom of people in the congregation who have expertise in fields related to wealth and poverty. It's also important to remember that the sermon doesn't have to do everything! Some practices can be more effectively presented and discussed in a congregational forum or an ongoing series on economic choices.
- Stories about alternative communities in developing countries can be eye-opening: what partnerships have been set up by your denomination to help people dig wells, set up co-ops for buying seeds, or involve women in decision-making? Stories like these, often told in denominational magazines and newsletters,

are waiting for the preacher to bring them off the page and into the pulpit.

- There are also powerful stories from communities within the United States. John Kretzmann and John McKnight have spent several years working in cities and towns across the United States. Their own "provocative alternative" is known as ABCD, or Asset Based Community Development, a process that begins with the *assets* of each community rather than the *needs*. In *Building Community from the Inside Out*, they tell hundreds of brief stories that provide provocative alternatives:
    - ➢ A local congregation creates a partnership with a nonprofit immigrant's support program...in which this church provides a nonthreatening atmosphere for recent immigrants while gaining greater contact with the various ethnic groups in the community.
    - ➢ A local church starts a construction company in order to bring affordable housing to the community. Because this church cannot afford to pay standard wages, it forms a partnership with the local prison in which prisoners are released each day to a local community college, and they get college credit for their construction work.[9]

It's often easier to point out problems than to envision new possibilities. Bearing the hard words isn't an end in itself for contemporary preachers any more than it was for the biblical prophets or for Jesus. Critique can open hearts and minds to the realities around us and to the dissonance between God's vision for the world and the way things are, but hard words aren't the last words, not for Isaiah or for Jesus. Isaiah warned the people of Israel about neglecting the poor and needy. He said they were like a rebellious tree and they would be cut down. Yet that was not the last word. Isaiah promised that the stump of that very tree would bring forth a shoot of green (Isa. 11:1). Zacchaeus, the tax collector in the sycamore tree, climbs down at Jesus' invitation. Zacchaeus gives half of his goods to the poor and promises fourfold payment to those he has defrauded. "Today salvation has come to this house," said Jesus, "because he too is a son of Abraham" (Luke 19:8-9). Even the hardest stones can come to life.

SERMON: WALKING AWAY FROM A LOVE STORY

Mark 10:17-31

Jesus, looking at him, loved him and said, "You lack one thing; go, sell what you own, and give the money to the poor, and you will have treasure in heaven; then come, follow me." When he heard this, he was shocked and went away grieving, for he had many possessions. (Mark 10:21-22)

Where did he go, that man who came to Jesus? Did he go to the bank to have the interest put into his passbook? Or to his estate on the edge of the city? Did he go to the high point on the hill overlooking his land? Where did he go, that man who came to Jesus?

He had come with eager expectation. He came running, interrupting Jesus' journey. He knelt before Jesus with a question that couldn't wait: "Good teacher, what must I do to inherit eternal life?" (Mark 10:17). In some ways it is an odd question. What must I *do* to *inherit* eternal life? Inheritance usually implies a gift: the oldest son inherits from the father simply because he is oldest, not because he has done anything. Had this man inherited something from his father? We don't know. At this point in the story, we don't even know he is rich. We only see him running and kneeling. And we know that he wants something he doesn't have. "Good teacher, what must I do to inherit eternal life?"

We have no reason to be suspicious of his motives. He hasn't come to trap Jesus on some intricate point of the law. This is *his* question, and he knows he can't answer it by himself. "Why do you call me good?" Jesus asks. "No one is good but God alone." But there is no time for the man to respond. We're left with our own questions: why was it wrong for this man to call Jesus "good"? Jesus *was* good, wasn't he? But Jesus has already gone on. "You know the commandments," and then he recites them, as we might have done in confirmation class. "You shall not murder; You shall not commit adultery; You shall not steal; You shall not bear false witness; You shall not defraud; Honor your father and mother" (Mark 10:18-19). Did the man notice anything unusual in the list? Did you? The order is a bit different, but Jesus has also added something: "You shall not defraud." Did the man hear that word? Did Jesus add it intentionally—perhaps suggesting that the man's wealth had come dishonestly? Did Jesus add it so we would know something about this man?

"Teacher, I have kept all these since my youth" (Mark 10:20). Since my bar mitzvah. Since confirmation. Since my youth, I have kept *all* of these commandments. Jesus doesn't argue with him: this man kneeling before him was a *good* man—good in the human sense. He had not murdered or commited adultery or stolen, and he had not defrauded anyone. At least that's what his answer implies—"I've kept *all* of these commandments." Note that Jesus doesn't dispute his answer. We need to remember that, for later, when we discover the man is rich, we may be tempted to say that his problem wasn't money, but fraud. There's nothing wrong with money, we may argue, except when it's *bad* money—but I'm getting ahead of the story.

For now it's enough for us to know that he was a good man and that his question about eternal life was real. But where did he go? By the end of the story, he has disappeared. The man who had come running and hoping, "went away grieving, for he had great possessions." This good man was shocked. He had answered Jesus honestly; he had kept the commandments since his youth. Jesus didn't challenge the man's answer, but Jesus didn't stop there. Jesus went on: "You lack one thing; go, sell what you own, and give the money to the poor, and you will have treasure in heaven; then come, follow me" (Mark 10:21).

You lack one thing. One thing. And this one thing cannot be earned or inherited. You lack one thing—but you must lack even more to find it! How strange it must have seemed to the good man. How strange, and how impossible. He was shocked and went away grieving. Where did he go, this good man who seemed to lack nothing? Where did he go?

He walked away from a love story because he could not walk away from his money. This *is* a story about money. But it is also a love story. Unfortunately, the love story can get lost in the midst of the money. No words are spoken, but the storyteller makes it plain. Before Jesus told the man to sell everything he owned, we *see* what is never spoken: "Jesus, looking at him, loved him." Jesus did not discount the man's question or his goodness; Jesus longed for this man to find what he was searching for. Jesus loved him, but knew how hard it would be for this good man to rest securely in that love. His security still rested in what he owned. He had a love affair with his possessions.

Was there room for goodness? Yes. Room for obedience? Yes. Perhaps there was even room for generosity. But there was no room for God's radical love story. "Why do you call me good?" Jesus asked the man. "Only God is good." Do you remember? When Jesus listed the commandments, he left out the first three. He mentioned only the commandments about loving your neighbor. But what about the first commandment, "I am the Lord your God. You shall have no other gods before me"? Why didn't Jesus ask the man about that commandment?

Or did he?

This good man came running to Jesus with a question from his heart: "What must I do to inherit eternal life?" When Jesus told him, he was shocked and went away grieving. As he turned his back on Jesus, he answered the unspoken question about loving God. He didn't answer with a word; he answered with his feet. He loved his possessions more than he loved God. Where did he go, that rich man? Perhaps he would look for eternal life in some other place.

Perhaps the man left hoping his possessions would become enough. Kathleen Norris talks about the gifts she has received in the barren places of far western South Dakota. In an area where there seems to be nothing for miles around, she has received the blessings of God. In a place where the towns grow smaller and smaller, her faith has grown larger than she ever imagined. And there, in her visits to a Benedictine monastery and in her daily living in a small Dakota town, this lapsed Presbyterian has reclaimed the faith she inherited. The farmers and the monks became her teachers:

> maybe looking to monks (who seek to live within limitations) as well as rural Dakotans (whose limitations are forced upon them by isolation and a harsh climate) can teach us how to live more realistically. These unlikely people might also help us overcome the

> pathological fear of death and the inability to deal with sickness and old age that plague American society.
>
> Consumerism is fed by a desire to forget our mortality.[10]

"Consumerism is fed by a desire to forget our mortality." Perhaps the good man would try to buy immortality. Perhaps meaning in his life would become even more dependent on money, and he would stop wondering about eternal life—whatever that had meant to him. He would try to believe the T-shirt that says, "WHOEVER HAS THE MOST TOYS WHEN HE DIES, WINS." But the greatest of all love stories would elude him. "Jesus, looking at him, loved him." Had the good man missed that look while trying so hard to answer the questions right? Did he fully hear what Jesus asked him to do—not only to go and sell, but also to *come and follow me?* Jesus was not asking this man to be a philanthropic hero, a loner commended for his generosity. Jesus was inviting this good man into an eternal love story that was beginning even now. This was God's love story, not reserved for some distant time and place, but a love story that would be known in community with Jesus and with other sisters and brothers—on earth as it is in heaven.

Where did he go, that good man? Scripture doesn't tell us. The story goes on without him. If we were tempted to forget about the money, though, Jesus won't drop the subject. "How hard it will be for those who have wealth to enter the kingdom of God!" (Mark 10:23)—more difficult than a camel squeezing through the eye of a needle. This *is* a story about money. Not bad money or junk bonds or failed savings and loans, not gambling or playing the numbers or cheating the poor—just money. It's a story about money. It's also a story about love rejected, about something so pervasive and all-possessing that it kept a good man from loving God with all his being and kept him from receiving God's love in his very bones. He went away grieving, perhaps hoping he could find a different answer somewhere else.

We'll never know if he did, but we do know he's not the only one looking. I see this searching all around me. Perhaps, you see it, too. It's the search by people who don't have to worry about putting food on the table or finding shelter in a refugee camp for themselves and their children. You can see the searching if you look through the lists of bestselling books. A few years ago these lists were topped by books about business and investment, about how to succeed and how to manage. A few of them still make the list. But something has changed. Now books on subjects such as angels are in the top ten on *The New York Times* paperback list. At one time, *The Care of the Soul,* a book about spirituality and daily life, was in first place. In second place was *The Road Less Traveled,* a book more about finding your life than making a living, and it had been on the bestseller list for 566 weeks! In the hardcover books, the nonfiction list was topped by *Embraced by the Light,* a book about a woman's near-death experience—it was on the list for 70 weeks. People may not be asking about eternal life, but thousands are yearning for immortality.

And for love. A fictional novel, *The Bridges of Madison County,* was on the bestseller list for 109 weeks. The nonfictional covered bridges of Madison County in my home state of Iowa have become something of a tourist attraction—like the cornfield baseball diamond from *Field of Dreams.* I haven't read the book about bridges. I only know it's the story of a photographer from the city who passes through Madison County. He falls in love with a farmer's wife, and she falls in love with him. Though they never see each other again after that brief encounter, it's a love affair that lasts a lifetime. And it spent 109 weeks on the bestseller list. Could it be that a lot of people are still searching for the love of their lives?

Where did he go, that rich man who came to Jesus? We will never know. But that isn't the only question, is it? Where will you go? Where will I? Though we may have food on the table and shelter over our heads, we probably don't consider ourselves rich. I know that many of us have a hard time throwing away the brown envelope from Publisher's Clearing House with our name printed next to "$1,000,000." There's something about money that is very compelling. Without thinking, we can easily fall in love with money. The dream of "having more" can capture our hearts and stir our imaginations.

Jesus knows this about us even as he knew the heart of the man who knelt down before him. We are seeking even as he was, looking for meaning large enough to hold us in the night when sleep won't come—and meaning has more to do with love than rational explanations. W. H. Auden asks questions about love in one of his "Twelve Songs":

> Will it come like a change in the weather?
> Will its greeting be courteous or rough?
>
> Will it alter my life altogether?
> O tell me the truth about love.[11]

The truth is—and the rich man knew it—the love of Jesus *would* alter his life altogether. Where did he go, that rich man who came to Jesus?

Where will I go, and you?

SERMON: AN EASY CHAIR IN THE LAUNDROMAT

Luke 16:19-31

Besides all this, between you and us a great chasm has been fixed, so that those who might want to pass from here to you cannot do so, and no one can cross from there to us. (Luke 16:26)

"What would you do if you won the lottery?" The pastor asked the question to a group of mothers in a church basement in Detroit. She had been their pastor for several years, living next door to the church in a neighborhood that was poorer by far than anyplace she had ever lived. Once a week, she met with this group of women. Some were raising their children alone, working when they could find jobs and someone to care for the kids. Some depended on welfare to keep a roof over their heads and food on the table. They doubled up in apartments with relatives when they had to; they passed on clothes from child to child. They shared at least two things in common: they were all Christians, and they were all poor.

"What would I do if I won the lottery?" one woman repeated the question, then offered an answer that made her face light up: "I'd buy easy chairs for the laundromat—enough chairs so everybody could sit down and take a load off. All they've got is three old chairs, and two have broken seats—and the one that's not broken is so hard you'd rather sit on a dryer and burn your—you know what I mean, Pastor." She laughed again, knowing there wasn't much she could say that would shock her pastor.

"That's it?" asked the pastor. "Easy chairs for the laundromat?" She had expected other answers: a bigger apartment, an exotic vacation, new furniture, perhaps a car. "It was just like them to think of the easy chairs," sh told me later. "They didn't even consider something just for themselves. They thought of all those women trudging into that grimy laundromat with no place to sit down and rest. I hear about poor women spending their money on fancy clothes or steaks, but I don't know any. The women I know would be grateful for a few decent chairs in the laundromat."

The answer surprised me, too, when I first heard the story. Maybe I couldn't appreciate the easy chairs because I don't spend much time in laundromats anymore. I just walk downstairs to the church basement and leave my laundry there, sloshing and sudsing, without watching or standing guard. If I have the time, I can go back upstairs to sit in an easy chair reading the paper while my clothes spin.

It was the utter simplicity of the easy chairs that struck me—and the notion that the imaginary windfall would be shared. There'd be enough chairs for *everybody* to take a rest. Perhaps I shouldn't have been surprised by this generous simplicity. What did I assume about poor women? What do poor women want? How often do I talk with women or men or children who are poor? Now I wouldn't call myself rich, but I do have a regular salary and a five-room apartment on the third floor of the church. I have a new used car and a checking account. I'm not poor, but I also know there are plenty of people who are wealthier than I am. I'm often flabbergasted by ads in the *New York Times*, and I ponder over them: Who would buy a $2,300 solid crystal turtle, and why? Or a $12,000 watch? Does it keep better time? Just seeing those ads makes me realize there are plenty of people far wealthier than I am, or who would be buying such things?

But there are many more people who are poor. Poorer, by far, than I am. I don't think I know many really rich people, but I also know that I don't spend much time with people who are poor. We may live in the same city, but we live in different worlds. There is a great chasm between me and those who are desperately poor. In the gospel reading, Jesus tells a parable that ends with two men dying. The rich man is in torment and wants the poor man to bring water to cool his tongue. But Abraham, cradling the poor man in his bosom, tells the rich man that "a great chasm has been fixed" between them. There is no way to get from here to there, or from there to here. A *great chasm* has been fixed: it was already there before the two men died.

Jesus paints the contrast in painfully clear images as the story begins:

> An unnamed rich man
>   *a poor man named Lazarus lying at his gate;*
> a rich man dressed in purple and fine linen
>   *a poor man covered with sores;*
> a rich man who feasted sumptuously
>   *a poor man who longed for crumbs from the rich man's table.*

There is no indication that the rich man knows Lazarus. Only the dogs pay attention to the poor man. Yet, when the rich man is in Hades, he calls out for Lazarus *by name.* He knew the poor man by name, but left him lying at his gate without even a crumb from his table.

Why? Why was there such a great chasm between the rich man and Lazarus *while they were alive?* We could quickly answer that the rich man was hard-hearted, selfish, and mean. Yet Jesus paints him as a man with great compassion for his family. From Hades, the rich man pleads with Abraham on behalf of his five brothers: don't let them come into this place of torment! But Abraham replies, "They have Moses and the prophets, they should listen to them" (Luke 16:29).

Here we come to the heart of the parable. What does it mean to listen to Moses and the prophets? Jesus is telling this parable to religious leaders who "have Moses and the prophets," but it was possible to read Moses and the prophets in many different ways. It was possible then, and it is possible now. The rich man could have believed he *was* following Moses and the prophets. Indeed, it may be true that his interpretation of the law *caused* the chasm between himself and Lazarus. It's possible that certain interpretations of scripture widen the great chasm in our own time.

Jesus is interpreting scripture with this parable. This is a story not only about economics, but also about theology. How do we rightly understand Moses and the prophets? Just read the Bible, some would say! But it's not so simple. In Deuteronomy 28:1, 2 we read these words: "If you will only obey the Lord your God. . . . These blessings shall come upon you." The verses that follow flesh out what these blessings include: blessings in city and field, fruits of the ground, increase in cattle and flocks, and on and on. Verse thirteen makes the promise abundantly clear: "The Lord will make you the head, and not the tail, you shall be only at the top, and not at the bottom—if you obey the commandments of the Lord your God." The rest of the chapter is filled with curses, curses that will come upon those who do not obey God's law.

These curses are direct reversals of the blessings: devastation and destruction, blight and mildew, pestilence and plague. Listen carefully to one particular curse: "The Lord will strike you on the knees and on the legs with grievous boils of which you cannot be healed, from the sole of your foot to the crown of your head" (Deut. 28:35).

"And at his gate lay a poor man named Lazarus, covered with sores...even the dogs would come and lick his sores" (Luke 16:20, 21). Jesus draws this picture carefully, precisely, calling attention to the sores. Lazarus looks exactly like the one who is cursed by God. Thus, according to *one* interpretation of Moses and the prophets, there *should* be a great chasm between poor Lazarus and the rich man. The rich man isn't called to do anything for the man lying at his gate, for poverty is a sign of God's punishment and disfavor. Poverty is the direct result of disobeying God.

But Jesus will not let this interpretation stand; indeed the parable argues directly against such an interpretation. Jesus knew there were other words in scripture. There was another way of reading the tradition. In the same book of Deuteronomy, we find these words: "You shall open your hand wide to your brother [and sister], to your poor and your needy" (Deut. 15:11 NKJV). This call for compassion is not a weak voice in scripture, but one that is steady and strong, reminding the people to leave grain in the fields for poor people, widows, and sojourners. The voice becomes even stronger in the writings of prophets such as Amos, Jeremiah, and Isaiah. Listen to Isaiah's words about true fasting:

> Is not this the fast that I choose: . . .
> Is it not to share your bread with the hungry,
> and bring the homeless poor into your house;
> when you see the naked, to cover them,
> and not to hide yourself from your own kin?
> (Isa. 58:6*a*, 7)

"And at his gate lay a poor man named Lazarus covered with sores." Which reading of Moses and the prophets will *we* choose when we see Lazarus lying at our gate?

It's no secret which reading Jesus chooses when he tells this parable: "The poor man died and was carried away by the angels to be with Abraham" (Luke 16:22). Poverty is not a sign of God's punishment—no matter what some parts of scripture say. And wealth is not a sign of obedience and faithfulness; the wealthy man was surely not blessed by Abraham.

Of course, Jesus didn't tell us exactly how to close the great chasm between rich and poor people. But it was clear that he thought there shouldn't be one here on earth. He told this parable to argue against any theology that sees poor people as undeserving outcasts condemned by God. If we listen closely to public conversations about poor people in our own country, we can hear the very theology Jesus argued *against.* Poor people are portrayed as guilty at every turn: they are lazy, they bear too many illegitimate children, they cheat the government, they lack motivation. Thus, they should be punished. Cut them off from Medicare. Drop them from the welfare rolls. Deny services to immigrants and their children. Widen the great chasm.

God knows there are no simple answers, and the mothers in the church basement will be among the first to tell us that welfare needs reforming. It will take wisdom from every quarter to find solutions and new directions to close the great chasm between rich and poor in this nation. It will take compassion and goodwill in measures large enough to overcome our fear. But more than that, we will need the living presence of Jesus to change our hearts and minds. You'd think that would be happening, for more and more voices claim to be speaking up for "Christian values." But is anybody speaking up for Lazarus? You and I know it's possible to find almost anything we want in scripture. If we look, we can find verses that proclaim wealth as God's blessing and poverty as God's curse. But the Hebrew prophets had a radically different vision. And so did Jesus Christ.

Those of us who claim to speak in Christ's name are called to share his vision—whether we are Lutherans or Methodists, Roman Catholics or Baptists, African

Methodist Episcopal Zion or members of the Christian Coalition. If we speak in the name of Jesus we must see Lazarus and love him, love him back to life again. We hardly know where to begin to close the chasm between the rich and the poor on this side of heaven. We could begin by talking to the women in the laundromat, and by listening—really listening—to the One who has risen from the dead.

CHAPTER FIVE

Splashing, Bursting Against the Stone

Meg Christian's song "The Rock Will Wear Away" begins with a question: "Can we be like drops of water/ Falling on the stone?"[1] The metaphor of raindrops on stone sings the possibility of small acts making a difference over time. Some stones carried from the Jordan remain as sentinels against amnesia, calling to mind the stories of God's deliverance from slavery and despair. Other stones, however, have become oppressive and God's word comes to break these stones in pieces. Or perhaps to reshape them with the gentle power of the falling rain.

Sometimes transformation happens suddenly: a moment of conversion, a vision that changes how life is seen, a word of forgiveness heard for the first time. Biblical transformation often seems like that—as immediate as the disciples' sudden decision to leave their fishing boats to follow Jesus. But the Bible also bears witness to transformation that doesn't happen suddenly; sometimes it takes days, weeks, or even years. Peter is called and leaves his boat at once, but often gets things wrong as he walks with Jesus. He confesses Jesus to be Messiah, then rebukes Jesus for talking about suffering and dying. He leaps out of the boat in faith, then begins to sink. He says he will follow Jesus everywhere, then denies even knowing him. At the very end of John's Gospel Jesus turns to Peter and says, "Follow me," as though the journey was just beginning. Peter the Rock is transformed again and again.

Transformational preaching takes place over time. There may be a rare life-changing sermon, but more often it is a lifetime of sermons inviting the listener into God's alternative vision that leads to transformation. Timing is important not only in crafting a single sermon but also in preaching Sunday after Sunday. This sense of timing may outline a plan for the Sundays of one church season or over an entire year. Preachers know there are difficult sermons that can be preached and heard after ten years in a congregation that would never have been heard when they first arrived.

Preaching for transformation calls for both *attentionality* and *intentionality.* The preacher *pays attention* to the members of the congregation, to faith commitments and traditions, to pain and hopes, to readiness to envision something new and resistance to anything that seems different. But the preacher is also *intentional,* planning for new understandings and moving carefully but deliberately into new territory. Beverly Harrison offers wise counsel when she says, "We often settle for being right rather than effectual, and people's lives depend on our being effectual."[2] Harrison isn't calling preachers to wait for a majority vote, but she knows the importance of not only speaking, but of being heard. The hope is for transformation, not alienation, and this is often a matter of timing.

Starting on Common Ground

Are there commonly held values that provide a place to stand together before moving into new territory? Has the preacher "exegeted" the congregation as carefully as the biblical texts to know what matters most to the listeners? Sociologist of religion Tex Sample has spent a good part of his career helping ministers understand different cultural groups within the United States. Experience has taught him that seminary-trained clergy have a particularly difficult time relating to people who are part of what he calls the "cultural right." Love of country is a high value for this group of people, but this isn't always true for clergy. Sample says, "I was taught in seminary to be very suspicious of the nation-state."[3]

He recalls a time he was invited to a congregation to preach a sermon about peace; the local pastor had told him to "lay it out" and preach from his heart. When he arrived on Saturday night, the pastor said, "By the way, Tex, this is really a 'hawk' church. Half the congregation is military, and the other half is a combination of skilled blue-collarites and low-middle-class sales and service people. I thought you might want to know that before tomorrow."[4] Of course Sample wished he had known before Saturday at 9:00 P.M., but he remembered an experience that reshaped his written text: a cross-country flight from Boston to Los Angeles on a cloudless, sun-filled day:

> In a matter of four or five hours—I can't remember how long, it seems an instant—I saw America from sea to shining sea. One simply cannot do that and not love this land. From Boston to L.A. across field and forest, lakes and mountains, deserts and plains....
>
> The next morning the sermon began with that story, and I used it to claim the beauty of other lands also, and the necessity of peace, the end of nuclear weapons, and the dream of a world without war.... Surely many people there disagreed with some, maybe most, of what I said, but they listened.... I made contact with *their* approach to meaning, with *their* love of country, and in that context they trusted me enough to let me say things they otherwise would not have tolerated gladly.[5]

Sample found common ground with the listeners that Sunday morning, working with only a late-hour clue from the resident pastor. He honored the country those parishioners held dear, yet he did not abandon the message he came to preach. Parish pastors have an advantage over Sample: they preach Sunday after Sunday to people they come to know deeply over time. Nevertheless, being in the same location is not sufficient if we aren't paying close attention to spoken and unspoken clues. How can those of us who preach be attentive to the values and worldview of a particular faith community?

- Go where people spend time: coffee shops, livestock barns, bowling alleys, high school ball games, laundromats, malls, playgrounds. Meet people in their workplaces. Take time to write about the experience: What did you see and hear? What brings delight or sorrow? How do people feel about their work and about themselves in their work?
- Listen to radio programs that are important to people (especially if it's not a program you would choose for yourself). Spend a week listening to country and western or hip-hop, talk radio, or evangelical Christian preachers. Watch television shows you know are popular with people in the congregation. Why wrestling? Why *Who Wants to Be a Millionaire* or *Touched by an Angel*?
- Make use of existing small groups to discern what people value: take time at a council meeting or Bible study to talk about work or family or money. Ask the confirmation class about their favorite music. Gather longtime church members to talk about "the old days" and the changes they've seen.

- Use a question box, bulletin insert, or e-mail to invite questions, concerns, and insights for a particular sermon series (for example, The Changing Roles of Women and Men, Immigrants and Other "Strangers," Growing Up Isn't What It Used to Be, and so on).

There are now many resources available from the field of congregational studies to aid pastors in "exegeting" a particular parish.[6] But there is still a need to pay close attention to conversations in homes and hospitals, in structured meetings and side conversations in the parking lot—lest the people become only part of a categorical box called "the Type B Congregation."

It's essential not only to be attentive but also to be intentional in making use of these insights for preaching. If country and western music represents the values of many in the congregation, how can preaching use these lyrics to help people think about relationships and family or about the meaning of work?[7] If you spend time at the mall, write down what you see. Take people to the mall in your sermon—walk from store to store, press your nose against the glass. What do we learn there about money and fashion, about community and loneliness? If the preacher can speak out of a deep understanding of commonly held values, it is far more likely that people will be open to an idea or teaching they hadn't considered before.

Moving On in Faith

I never met my great-grandfather Hemborg, but I've seen his picture many times: a distinguished-looking Lutheran pastor with a wondrous handlebar mustache. My grandmother once told me that no congregation would ever have called a pastor who didn't have a mustache. (Obviously this was long before the ordination of women!) Having or not having a mustache may seem a very insignificant issue on the stage of history, but fear of change is far from insignificant.

It's critical to help people see that change does not mean erosion of the faith or the destruction of deep values. Christian traditions are filled with stories of change—not change for the sake of change, but for the sake of the gospel. The Hebrew prophets called people to examine their hearts and move from empty worship to a deeper concern for the poor and needy outside the temple doors (Jeremiah). Jesus called people to change their long-held traditions about who could eat together. Martin Luther called the Catholic Church to change its teachings about grace and salvation. Abolitionists of the 1800s called people not only to change their hearts but also to give up an economic system that depended on slave labor. And sometime in the early part of the 1900s, my grandmother's congregation came to understand that one's gifts for ministry did not depend on having a mustache.

Most congregations include stories in archives or communal memories about changes made in order to be faithful to God's calling in a particular time in history: a merger between two struggling congregations that enabled ministry to survive and even thrive, a decision to stay in the city when the neighborhood went through racial transition, or the commitment to resettle displaced people after World War II. While it's true that not every change is for the sake of the gospel, neither is every change heresy.

Standing on common ground with the congregation, the preacher asks, "Where is God calling us in this time of history?" or "How can we be faithful to Jesus' call to welcome the stranger today?" or "What new truth is the Holy Spirit leading us to discover in this generation?"

Splashing, Bursting Against the Stone: Sexuality as a Case Study

> "Teacher, this woman was caught in the very act of committing adultery. Now in the law Moses commanded us to stone such women. Now what do you say?" (John 8:4-5)

The religious leaders had come to Jesus with stones in their hands, stones bearing the weight of tradition and words written down. Why did they bring the woman and not the man—he must have been there, for she was "caught in the very act"? And why adultery? Why not a landowner who treated his tenants unjustly or a rich man who refused to care for widows and orphans? Were sexual sins considered the worst of all sins, and thus provided the best opportunity for trapping Jesus? "Let anyone among you who is without sin be the first to throw a stone at her," Jesus said (John 8:7*b*). When he looked up they had all gone away, but the text doesn't tell us if they dropped the stones or kept them in their hands. Indeed, the stone throwers seem to return in every generation, rounding up those accused of sexual sins. Though the church calls sexuality a gift from God, this "gift" has more often been condemned than cherished.

As we enter the twenty-first century, the subject of sexuality, and particularly homosexuality, is tearing the church apart. There seems to be very little common ground on which to stand and more than enough fear to silence preachers completely. Nonetheless, sexuality is not going away. Sexuality affects our feelings about our bodies, as well as gender roles and families. Sexuality has been at the center of politics from impeachment trials to campaign platforms. Sexuality has been studied by almost every denomination in the United States over the past decade and continues to be on the agenda of many churchwide conventions and assemblies.

How can we find common ground?

In some ways, our common ground seems obvious: we are all sexual beings. But once we have said that, the conversation gets more difficult. Is there any other common ground on which to stand?

Embarrassment. We laughed at jokes we didn't understand in junior high. We couldn't imagine that our parents ever had a sexual relationship (we must have gotten here some other way). We worried in high school about being masculine or feminine enough (and now even those rules seem to have changed). Our parents talked about "it" without using the word "sex" or handed us a little book (and we aren't much better talking to our own children). This is one piece of common ground: we're embarrassed. Admitting that can be a place to begin.

Advertising images. What do commercials tell us about what it means to be a man or woman? What do shapely dolls and muscle-bound action figures say about girls and boys? What do sexual-enhancement products say about men and women, sexuality, and aging? This can be another point of common ground: we share media space, a space saturated with sexual messages.

Family. Even if our version of family is idealized or our experience of family has been harmful, we still have a sense that family is important. Novelist Roxana Robinson explains why her stories often center on the family:

> The family is at the heart of our emotional lives. It's where the heat is, the source of our most powerful feelings.
>
> Family connections ... form the strongest bonds we will ever know. These are the people who make us happier, and angrier, than anyone else on earth. And these connections are indestructible: you might reject your family members, you might refuse to see them ever

> again, but they will still be your family. You will always be a part of them, whether you choose to be or not.[8]

The importance of family can be an area of common ground from which the preacher explores biblical families, new definitions of family, and the possibility of dangerous families (child abuse, incest, domestic violence).

The Bible. Scripture may not seem like common ground at all since people interpret the Bible in wildly divergent ways. Yet the Bible is a place for preacher and congregation to stand together, for it claims a unique space as the book of the church. In most congregations, the Bible bears authority far greater than the American Psychiatric Association or the most respected studies on sexual abuse. Preacher and congregation may disagree on what the authority of scripture means, but the Bible remains a shared space. If the authority of scripture is understood as the inerrancy of the literal words, how is it possible to set some literal words aside but insist on the authority of others? What do the literal words of scripture tell us about families? (Abraham, Sarah, Hagar, Ishmael, and Isaac may not fit our picture of a traditional family. Is there any biblical family that models "Christian values"?) How do we understand Jesus' teachings on divorce in light of abusive or unfaithful marriages? What do we do with Jesus' words that redefine "family" almost every time he uses the word? The Bible can provide common ground, even with uncommon understandings.

Common ground will differ from one congregation to another. There are also differences *within* a congregation: people may be at very different places in talking about sexuality, in their feelings about family, and in their interpretation of the Bible. Listening to these different voices is critically important. It will be almost impossible for people to reconsider long-held values if they feel they have been disregarded or dismissed.

Why would we venture beyond our common ground?

Why not stay where we are in our understanding of human sexuality? Why should anyone consider changing values held for a lifetime? These questions are critical, for transformational preaching isn't about change for its own sake but change in light of God's call to people in every generation. Do the stones of tradition continue to give life, or have they become rigid and even harmful?

For centuries the church was silent about domestic violence and sexual abuse. Some would go farther than that and charge the church with condoning violence and abuse in order to uphold marriage, family privacy, or clergy status. But it is possible to be wrong for a long time. In recent years, preachers have broken silence and have spoken out about topics like sexual abuse and incest. It is not unusual for a pastor to share a story about preaching on domestic violence on Sunday and receiving a call from an abused woman on Monday. Breaking silence can be the beginning of transformation and healing.

Some have discovered scripture as a resource for celebrating sexuality as part of God's good creation. This is indeed transforming news to people who have grown up believing that sex is shameful. From early childhood I listened as our pastor began worship with the "Confession of Sins" printed in the Lutheran service book: "Almighty God, our Maker and Redeemer, we poor sinners confess unto Thee, that we are *by nature sinful and unclean . . .*" (emphasis added).[9] Was I the only person in the sanctuary who thought "sinful and unclean" meant sex rather than greed or sloth? In her commentary on Song of Songs, Ellen Davis affirms the surprising mutuality between the woman and the man singing to each other in the garden: "This is the only place in the Bible where the love between man and woman is treated without concern for childbearing or the social and political benefits of marriage."[10] They simply delight in each other and aren't afraid to include each other's bodies in their celebration. Like Davis, Old Testament scholar Phyllis Trible also delights in the passionate mutuality of the Song, calling it "a symphony of love":

> Born to mutuality and harmony, a man and a woman live in a garden where nature and history unite to celebrate the one flesh of sexuality. Naked without shame or fear (cf. Gen. 2:25; 3:10), this couple treat each other with tenderness and respect. Neither escaping nor exploiting sex, they embrace and enjoy it. . . . Testifying to the goodness of creation, then, eroticism becomes worship in the context of grace.[11]

Though the Song is seldom included in the lectionary readings, it may be time to get beyond our embarrassment and start singing it once again. The passionate mutuality of the Song is long overdue, as Bishop Krister Stendahl reminds us: "While the church traditionally has been forceful in teaching fidelity, the church's record on mutuality has been weak indeed."[12] Sexuality has shaped and continues to shape every person at worship: the teenager pressured to prove himself or herself sexually, the single adult longing for intimacy, the fifty-year-old man worried about growing old, the couple whose daughter just came out to them as a lesbian, the single mother who's never been married, the faithful church member upset about the denomination's "obsession" with homosexuality—the list is as long as the names in the church directory.

Transformational preaching in the area of human sexuality might include the following:

- Celebrating the goodness of sexuality and challenging the negative teachings from the Christian tradition, for they are heavy stones to carry.
- Taking away the deep shame connected with sexuality since childhood.
- Breaking silence about domestic violence, incest, and sexual abuse.
- Ending discrimination and violence against gay men and lesbian women.
- Valuing different kinds of families in the congregation and community.
- Affirming single people as whole human beings, not "lesser halves" or "have-nots."
- Testing the biblical texts about homosexuality as a scribe trained for the kingdom of heaven, bringing both old and new as resources for faithful discernment.[13]
- Helping women and men cherish their bodies: we have very few hymns or liturgical resources that give thanks for our physical bodies—perhaps sermons can be a place to start.
- Honoring fidelity *and* mutuality as ethical norms for all committed, intimate relationships (both straight and gay).

Some people will be open to consideration of all these possibilities. Some will be uncomfortable, even resistant, to most of them. The pastor who has come to know people in the parish is the best resource for determining where to begin transformational conversations.

A series of sermons on sexuality might be preached four Sundays in a row or spaced out over a year's time. These sermons might be shaped by appointed lectionary readings or by biblical texts chosen by the preacher. Some texts written in stone will be tested by human experience and new understandings of human sexuality. (It's amazing to remember that the ovum wasn't discovered until the 1800s. This new understanding meant that a pregnant woman was no longer seen only as an incubator carrying the nascent life created solely by a man.)

Whatever preaching plan is chosen, it's essential to be *attentive* to the voices within the congregation and to the Holy Spirit who continues to be our tutor, leading us into fuller truth. It's equally essential to be *intentional*, to move through resistance toward life-giving transformation. Such intentionality is vitally important, for the stones of traditional teachings about human sexuality have caused grave harm over the centuries. These heavy stones continue to demean and diminish many people, both gay and straight, in our congregations and in the larger community.

But what about tradition's stones carried from the river? What about the words of the Bible? While texts about wealth and poverty have often been tested and reinterpreted, texts about sexuality seem to be written in stone. Something strange happens in the story of Joshua at the river. After the people crossed over the Jordan, after the twelve stones were set up in the camp, the text includes this little verse set in parentheses: "(Joshua set up twelve stones in the middle of the Jordan, in the place where the feet of the priests bearing the ark of the covenant had stood; and they are there to this day)" (Josh. 4:9).

Were the stones carried *from* the river or set up *in* the river? Perhaps two different traditions came together, and both were remembered. It may be confusing, but it's a wondrous reminder that scripture is not tidy. Twelve stones carried from the river and twelve stones set up in the river. The text tells us this second set of stones is still there—under the water. Surely those stones have been reshaped and rearranged since Joshua's day! Over time, God's living water will wear away the heavy stones of condemnation, fear, and shame, and new life will spring up where the rock had been.

SERMON: NO SMALL THING

1 Samuel 20:12-23, 35-42

Jonathan made David swear again by his love for him; for he loved him as he loved his own life. (1 Samuel 20:17)

Many summers ago, two fifth-grade girls came running up to me just before our outdoor worship service began. Breathless, they burst out with the news: that very afternoon the two of them had become blood sisters under the maple tree in the Johnsons' backyard. They had pledged loyalty and love to each other—a Lutheran and a Roman Catholic (they told me that, too)—and they wanted me to say a prayer for them in the service.

Such pledges of friendship are not uncommon for children. Adults smile, knowing "forever" may only mean until Saturday. But forever meant forever to those two girls that night in July. Their strong feelings for each other were real, for they had not yet learned that girls shouldn't show too much affection toward each other. Boys hadn't yet been scared into keeping an arm's length from their friends. But early, very early, we are taught demeaning labels that warn us not to take friendship too seriously. So we wave a nostalgic farewell to the blood sisters and brothers of childhood, leaving them behind under the maple trees of summer. We tell ourselves it's time to grow up.

David and Jonathan were friends for childhood's time. If you went to Sunday school you might remember how the Sunday school teacher "walked" David and Jonathan across the flannel board with quivers of arrows on their backs. The teacher talked about friendship, about how good it was to have friends to play with—but no one read the story to us in confirmation class. Adults have put away the Sunday school leaflets of David and Jonathan, replacing them with David's psalms. We've gone on to other things, and if we go back to the old story, we are almost embarrassed at the words on the page: "Jonathan made David swear again by his love for him; for he loved him as he loved his own life." It was a good story in grade school, but better passed over in the adult class or in sermons. We must hurry on to talk about more important issues, more "normal" relationships.

Yet scripture has preserved this story as one of the most beautiful pictures of human love. In many ways this is hard to explain. Coming from a culture that valued procreation and saw God's promise made real in descendants, there was little reason to keep such a story of friendship between two men. Whatever the reason for this story's survival, we can give thanks that the scribes didn't abandon it like a worn-out Sunday school leaflet. This story comes to us now when we're grown up and invites us to celebrate and honor those with whom we once dared to be under the trees of summer, when promises of friendship were forever.

This loving story speaks to deep needs and longings in the human spirit that are touched by God's word. This is a word that reaches us where we are vulnerable and often afraid, a word that embraces both passion and promise as God's gifts to human beings. "In the beginning is the relation"—that's what Jewish theologian Martin Buber once said.[14] Not just creation but relation: God who longed not only to be, but to-be-with. The God of creation is a passionate God. We've lost that early innocence that lets us speak of God's passion. Like Adam and Eve, we cover ourselves and speak instead of God's compassion. That word is not so naked, and we can say it without blushing. We've learned that passion is something to be controlled, no longer gift but vice. So it is that much of the church's teaching throughout history emphasized that the only reason for passion was procreation. Such teachings lead us not only to think that birth control is wrong but that passion itself is wrong. Such teachings also limit passion to sexual activity. That was never God's idea! Passion is that well of the spirit in which tears, as well as ecstasy, are born. Rage and weeping do not come from our head but from some more mysterious source. Indeed, it seems true that passion—not procreation—is uniquely human among God's gifts. While procreation is indeed a gift, it is given to giraffes and gerbils as well as to human beings. But passion, in all its fullness, goes beyond the mating cycles and is not bound by the need to reproduce ourselves.

The story of David and Jonathan is a very passionate story. Yes, it is compassionate, but surely it is also passionate. The feelings these two friends have for one another cannot be expressed in a handshake or a slap on the back. Later on in this chapter, they meet secretly outside the city to see each other for the last time. It has become clear that King Saul means to kill David out of jealousy, and Jonathan has shot arrows as a signal to tell David it is no longer safe for him to return to the court:

> David rose from beside the stone heap and prostrated himself with his face to the ground. He bowed three times, and they kissed each other, and wept with each other; David wept the more. Then Jonathan said to David, "Go in peace, since both of us have sworn in the name of the LORD, saying, 'The LORD shall be between me and you, and between my descendants and your descendants, forever.' " (1 Sam. 20:41-42)

These two friends didn't need a touchdown as reason for embrace. They simply loved each other beyond words. Period.

Not long ago I was very moved while watching the televised reports of the anniversary of D day. As taps played out over the Normandy beach, grown men stood weeping on the hillside. In broken voices they remembered names of friends buried among the endless rows of white markers. Must men see their buddies die before they dare to weep? Is it only war that makes friendship "forever"? Must we always say, "Oh, he's just a friend" to qualify the love we feel for another? Friendship is one of God's most passionate gifts to us—grown-ups as well as children.

Still, there is something more that must be said about this friendship between Jonathan and David. This is a story not only of passion but also of promise. It's a story promising friendship unto death and beyond, a promise that is remembered and honored as the story unfolds. After Jonathan's death in battle, David takes Jonathan's little crippled son into his own household. They become family though they are not related.

Is it only accidental that several stories in scripture point to promises made beyond family and bloodline? Ruth, a woman from Moab, is sealed in a covenantal promise with her widowed mother-in-law, Naomi: "Your people shall be my people" (Ruth 1:16*b*). Jonathan, the son of a king, pledges his love to David, the shepherd boy, "for he loved him as he loved his own life." And on that day when the sky grew dark, Jesus looked down from the cross at his closest friend saying, "Behold, your mother," and to his mother Mary, "Woman, behold your son" (John 19:26-27 NKJV). From that day they became family. In the Bible, where long lists of "begats" trace lineage and family tree, these stories in which water is thicker than blood remain as signs of the validity of promises born in love.

Do we take such promises seriously in our own lives? I have often seen the life-giving wonder of friendship during my years as a parish pastor. A man whose life has been filled with tragedy lives out the promise of friendship with a woman who is going blind too early. Together they go shopping, balance checkbooks, and work in the church garden. They are "just friends," they would say, but I would trust that promise of friendship and caring as surely as a marriage vow. I see a middle-aged man going to the hospital every day to visit his partner of many years. Both men are actors, encouraging each other in their craft. One supported the other through a life-threatening illness years ago. They are two men who love each other passionately, whose promises to each other have lasted through sickness and health, for richer and for poorer.

"To take a vow is an awful risk," wrote Sam Keen.[15] But so is never taking any vow at all. Without a vow love cannot deepen and flourish. "If the relationship is always contingent, on trial, the persons involved are too busy reassuring themselves for delight to develop."[16] These are good words for a marriage service; they are good words also for those we call "friends." The promise Jonathan and David made to each other is that kind of deep promise—a promise reserved, perhaps, for only a few friends in a lifetime. Such depth comes only through making and keeping promises. It will never come at all if we cannot bring ourselves to take friendship seriously.

I haven't seen those two fifth-grade girls in years. Perhaps they've forgotten the promise made under the maple tree of summer. If they have forgotten, I hope they've found others to call friend. I hope that sometime in their lives they've heard a sermon that lifted up friendship as a treasure. I hope they've marked the anniversary of a friendship as surely as they have celebrated other anniversaries in their lives. I wish for them lives enriched by the passion and promise of friendship. If that hasn't happened in a long time, I invite them—and you—back into a story of childhood, a story of two men who loved each other passionately. Two friends who made promises to each other before God that lasted beyond death. David and Jonathan, tell us again and again how much you loved each other. Help us this day to cry, to laugh, to embrace, and to say, "I love you" to a friend. Help us to know that this, too, is a promise and a passion born of God.

SERMON: LOOSING IS NOT LOSING

Matthew 18:15-20

Truly I tell you, whatever you bind on earth will be bound in heaven, and whatever you loose on earth will be loosed in heaven. (Matthew 18:18)

By now many of you have heard this Gospel reading three times in as many days. It was the appointed Gospel for this past Sunday and the central text for yesterday's worship. By the end of this service, perhaps you'll have it memorized! This section of Matthew 18 is often called "The Rule for Discipline"; it is probably more accurate to call it "The Rule for Reconciliation." Either way, it is a word spoken to the church: *ecclesia*—a word that is particular to Matthew and used by no other Gospel writer. Here the disciples—and by extension the church—are called to the ministry of binding and loosing: "Truly I tell you," said Jesus, "whatever you bind on earth will be bound in heaven, and whatever you loose on earth will be loosed in heaven." If you've taken a course on the Gospel of Matthew (or if you know this Gospel inside out!), you'll remember that we've heard these words before. In Matthew 16:18-19, Jesus speaks these words to Peter alone:

> And I tell you, you are Peter, and on this rock I will build my church [*There's that word again!*] and the gates of Hades will not prevail against it. I will give you the keys of the kingdom of heaven, and whatever you bind on earth will be bound in heaven, and whatever you loose on earth will be loosed in heaven.

Some have insisted that there's a big difference between Jesus' words to Peter and his later words to the disciples. The words to Peter are about right teaching, while the words to the disciples are about church discipline.[17] But does this distinction between teaching and discipline really matter? Why have people been disciplined by the church? Through the centuries people have been *disciplined* by the church for disobeying the *teachings* of the church. Right teaching and discipline have been intertwined throughout church history; it was true for Copernicus and Galileo as well as the witches in Salem.

Binding and loosing are rabbinic terms that are defined as the authority to declare something forbidden or allowed and the authority to inflict or lift a ban. " 'Binding and loosing on earth as in heaven' means interpreting former expressions of God's will . . . so as to show 'what is fitting for now' in a specific situation of the church's experience."[18]

Let me bring these definitions down to earth a bit. Come with me back to the middle of the nineteenth century—to the discovery of anesthesia and a great debate. The debate wasn't about appendectomies or amputations; it was about this question: Should anesthesia be given to a woman in severe labor pain, pain that threatened her life and the life of her child? The dilemma centered on Genesis 3, verse 16: "To the woman [God] said, 'I will greatly increase your pangs in childbearing; in pain you shall bring forth children.' " Some asked, "What right do we as mortals have to set aside God's word?" Others responded, "What right do we have to keep women in pain?" Medical journals in this country and in Great Britain published the arguments for both sides, pro and con.

The debate wasn't waged primarily in theological seminaries but among Christian medical doctors. The doctors pored over Hebrew lexicons, struggling to be faithful to their calling as Christians and as healers. It seemed that the Hebrew text supported those who opposed anesthesia. But someone on the other side, also appealing to scripture, argued that God was the first anesthesiologist, putting Adam to sleep in order to create Eve! Over time, anesthesia became available to women to ease debilitating labor pains. The journals don't record a vote on the matter, but medical practice changed.[19]

How did this change happen? Not through careful exegesis of the Hebrew words. The text says what it says. Does God want women to have the most pain possible?

Should we then *increase* a woman's pain in labor?[20] Does the church care for men more than for women? It might seem so since church teachings have paid little heed to the next verses spoken to the man: "Cursed is the ground because of you; in toil you shall eat of it all the days of your life. . . . By the sweat of your face you shall eat bread" (Gen. 3:17*b*, 19*a*). How could men sweat for their bread while driving an air-conditioned tractor? Or were words spoken to women binding while words to men were not?

How did this shift happen? Perhaps those who supported anesthesia appealed to love of neighbor as a greater good than one verse spoken at the edge of the garden. They loosed the authority of Genesis 3:16*a* in order to be *faithful* to a greater commandment.

Moving out of Genesis to the texts we heard at the beginning of our worship:[21] Do we insist that those with skin diseases live outside the camp, unclean and ostracized forever (see Leviticus 15:45-46)? When Nelson Mandela protested South Africa's apartheid regime, should he have been bound by Paul's words in Romans 13, verse 1: "those authorities that exist have been instituted by God"? What of the words in 1 Timothy: "I permit no woman to teach or to have authority over a man" (2:12)? That verse eliminates half of our faculty and more than half of the student body at Union!

Some of you already sense where I'm going—the issue that is tearing the church apart in our time: homosexuality. Almost every denomination in this country has spent hours, months, even years debating the subject. I know many people wish this whole debate would go away! I often wish this debate would go away, too. Then I remember the words of our departed sister Audre Lorde: "Sometimes we are blessed with being able to choose the time and the arena and the manner of our revolution, but more usually we must do battle wherever we are standing."[22]

This is where we are standing. This is a revolution for our time in history. The task of binding and loosing has been entrusted to the church—to us. As I have listened to the ongoing church debates about homosexuality, one thing has become abundantly clear: *We have reached an exegetical impasse.* Leviticus 18:22 says what it says—in Hebrew as well as English. If we set that verse aside as part of an archaic holiness code, we still must deal with Romans 1:26-27. Did Paul have any concept of what we now call "homosexual orientation"? Some will turn to 1 Corinthians 6 and its list of vices. But how many times can we exegete the Greek words *malakoi* and *arsenokoitoi* (1 Cor. 6:9-10)? We are stuck. We cannot live by exegesis alone.

But we are called to live by the word of God—a word so close that we bind it upon our foreheads and write it on our doorposts and our gates. As people of God, we are bound in a covenant relationship. I am bound to love God with heart, soul, mind, and strength and to love my neighbor as myself. I believe we are bound to care for the widow and the orphan and to welcome the stranger and the sojourner, for these words rise up again and again in scripture like an underground river springing to the surface whenever we are tempted to forget.

Jesus didn't shy away from this rabbinical task of binding and loosing. We hear him teaching in the repeated pattern of the Sermon on the Mount: "You have heard that it was said . . . but I say to you." Sometimes Jesus *binds* the law more expansively than tradition had: "You have heard that it was said to those of ancient times, 'You shall not murder. . . . ' But I say to you that if you are angry with a brother or sister, you will be liable to judgment" (Matt. 5:21-22*a*). At other times, Jesus *looses* traditional interpretations: "You have heard that it was said, 'An eye for an eye and a tooth for a tooth.' But I say to you, Do not resist an evildoer" (Matt. 5:38-39*a*). "You have heard that it was said, 'You shall love your neighbor and hate your enemy.' But I say to you, Love your enemies and pray for those who persecute you" (Matt. 5:43-44).

Jesus entrusted this ministry of binding and loosing to the church. He must have known it would be necessary—or why would he have established this ministry within the church? Jesus knew questions would arise in every generation, questions the Bible does not address—whether they are about anesthesia or homosexual orientation. However, for many people homosexuality is the place where Christians must hold the line. On this issue we must insist on a literal and inerrant interpretation of the Bible: *We set aside Genesis 3:16 when doctors gave anesthesia to women in labor; we overturned the words of 1 Timothy 2 when women were ordained; and we loosed the authority of Ephesians 6 when we insisted that slaves be freed. But this is the line in the sand: if we loose the texts condemning homosexuality we will lose the Bible and our faith.*

I received an insight into this dilemma from my computer. As I typed the words *binding* and *loosing*, my computer flagged *loosing* as misspelled. I removed one *o* to make the word *losing*—the squiggly red line went away, and all was well. *But loosing is not the same as losing.* It is possible to *loose* an oppressive teaching without *losing* the word of God. Indeed, there are times when it is the faithful thing to do. This is our calling as a community of theologians: to help people struggle with biblical texts, to assure them that we stand in a long line of believers who have loosed certain texts for faithful reasons. To help people in our church communities see that loosing does not mean losing.

Wait—there is something else: we never do this work alone. Binding and loosing can only be done in the presence of the One who called us to this ministry, the One who promised, "For where two or three are gathered in my name, I am there among them" (Matt. 18:20).

Jesus, even now in the midst of us. Jesus, assuring us that loosing is not losing.

Conclusion
Living Stones

It is by the ongoing enterprise of religious and scholarly communities that the text lingers over time in available ways. Out of that lingering, however, from time to time, words of the text characteristically erupt into new usage. They are seized upon by someone in the community with daring. Or perhaps better, the words of the text seize someone in the community who is a candidate for daring. In that moment of re-utterance, the present is freshly illuminated, reality is irreversibly transformed.[1]

Like stones set up for remembrance, the text lingers over time. Words are passed down to the children's children so the story will not be forgotten. "What do these stones mean?" It is an old question, yet it is always new. The preacher reads the text that has been read for centuries in other places among other people, yet the preacher listens as though the text has never been heard in quite this way before. This is the mystery of preaching: to hear a text that lingers, and still be surprised by words that explode.

After preaching years of Easter sermons I cannot tell you why I was caught off guard by the angel sitting on the stone. Perhaps it was a sudden recollection of Tomie dePaola's painting of that angel on a children's calendar. Perhaps it was the sight of gravestones rising from the sidewalks in the South Bronx. Perhaps it was walking among the tombstones in an Iowa cemetery after my father died. The lingering text spoke from the silent page, evoking images and memories, touching deep sadness and loss. This is the mystery of God's Spirit breathing life into the stones of scripture, making connections, and enlivening memory.

The preacher comes to the text expectantly—without files from last Easter, without downloaded printouts of other preachers' sermons, without commentaries (perhaps they will be opened later). If possible, the preacher listens while someone else reads the text aloud to hear it as others will the next Sunday. Or the preacher intentionally reads from an unmarked Bible—one without notes in the margins or key words underlined. After years of preaching, how can we hear the words as though for the first time? How can the words of the text "seize" us if we're already certain what the text means? Certainties can block a new hearing and preempt the Spirit's transforming power.

I caught a glimpse of this on a human scale years ago as a new pastor in New York City. In my first month in the parish, I climbed on a bus with several elderly women from the congregation; all of us were on our way to a meeting of the Lutheran Church Women. I felt positively young among them—being only thirty-six at the time—because most of them were twice my age! As we bounced along I turned to Clara, my seatmate, and asked her when she had come to this country and how long she had been a member of the congregation. After a few minutes I asked what I had wanted to ask her all along: "Do you ever think about moving away from New York?" (For I assumed she would if she could.) "Oh, no, Pastor Loondblatt," Clara answered, turning my Swedish name to German, "I would never leave New York. If I lived anywhere else, I would be in prison."

She went on to tell me how she loved to ride the bus and the subway. "You can get all the way to Far Rockaway beach for one token," she said. "How could I live any place else without a car? I would be in prison." I think she repeated the word for my benefit. I had assumed New York City *was* a prison for Clara and the others. My assumptions about older women and the city weren't yet written in stone, but they could have hardened fast without Clara. That conversation was one of many reminders that the preacher needs to be transformed.

The text sits beside us like a conversation partner on the bus. Will we be open to a new hearing? Will the Spirit surprise us, saying, "Look again! You missed the angel sitting on the stone"? The preacher doesn't sit alone with the text—even when no one else is in the room. Clara is there, too, along with the others on the bus and the younger ones who are at work or school. The Spirit hovers over the lingering text and beckons a conversation with the preacher and with those who will hear the words in the midst of worship. This particular conversation has never happened before: this text speaking to this preacher and these people in this time and place. Through such Spirit-born conversation, God is at work transforming memory into presence. "What has been *tradition,* hovering in dormancy, becomes available *experience.*"[2]

The stones set up as monument and reminder come to life: "Come to [Jesus Christ], a living stone, though rejected by mortals yet chosen and precious in God's sight, and like living stones, let yourselves be built into a spiritual house" (1 Peter 2:4-5*a*).

The Epistle writer turns to us where we are sitting and says, "Let yourselves be built into a spiritual house," or "You yourselves are being built," according to other manuscripts. Either way, the text doesn't say, "Build a spiritual house" as though we're doing it on our own. *Let yourselves be built.* It was often hard to remember those words in the fieldstone church on Bennett Avenue in New York City. The cornerstone was etched with the date 1928, marking the age not only of the stones but of the boiler as well. As many urban pastors (and probably many others) know, it's easy to be consumed with buildings—from boilers designed for coal to aging slate roofs nobody knows how to repair. It's also tempting to be obsessed with numbers—as in the unfortunate expression, "We worship about twelve hundred on Sundays." (Is God included among the twelve hundred?)

But this house of living stones is not our own doing: Jesus Christ is the cornerstone of this breathing building, shaping and reshaping us into a community different from one we would build by ourselves. The Epistle moves toward liturgy as we imagine the congregation joining in antiphonal response:

> Once you were not a people,
> *but now you are God's people;*
> once you had not received mercy,
> *but now you have received mercy.*
> (1 Peter 2:10, emphasis added)

Once more we gather at the river, touching the stones of remembrance. We rehearse our parts in God's alternative script, practicing words and actions that may transform the way we live beyond the sanctuary doors. The words of liturgy linger: *Kyrie eleison, Christe eleison, Kyrie eleison.* They are ancient words, yet at times they erupt with the particular voices and faces of the men, women, and children singing in the sanctuary: "For this holy house and for those who offer here their worship and praise, let us pray to the Lord: *Lord, have mercy.*"[3]

The Spirit hovers over the words of worship book and Bible, over the one who speaks, and over those who listen. We pray that the winds of the Spirit will transform the lingering text into living words. This prayer is not only for the sermon but also for the confession and words of forgiveness, the hymns and spoken litanies, the eucharistic prayer, and the altar call. May words that harm or demean be transformed by the Spirit's power, bringing life where the rock had been. "Gracious God, in your mercy, *hear our prayer.*" The Spirit blesses silence as well as speech and moves our bodies to dance and shout and cry. Transformation in worship affects hearts as well as heads. We experience reconciliation in the embrace of peace even when we don't know the other's name. We taste God's grace at the communion table even if the sermon has missed us.

After the feast, pastor and people are sent forth, giving thanks and praying that God's alternative script will transform their lives:

> In gratitude, in deep gratitude
> for this moment,
> this meal,
> these people,
> we give ourselves to you.
>
> Take us out
> to live as changed people
> because we have shared the Living Bread
> and cannot remain the same.[4]

This prayer gathers up the bread broken at the table and the living bread of scripture and sermon. The preacher prays and Clara prays, along with the whole breathing body of living stones:

- We pray that God's living word will feed us with grace as real as "bread in the pockets of the hungry."[5]
- We pray that God will keep calling stones to life, reshaping us into a community beyond our own making.
- We pray that Jesus will teach us to be scribes trained for the commonwealth of heaven, and that we will test what is written so that when the children ask for bread, we will not give them a stone.

- We pray that the Spirit will give us courage to hear and bear the hard words that call pastor and people to live Jesus' provocative alternatives.
- We pray through Sundays and seasons that the Spirit will breathe upon rocks grown rigid that we may become a house of living stones.

Long ago an angel descended from heaven and rolled away the huge stone that sealed the tomb. Then the angel sat down, transforming the stone of death into a resurrection pulpit. Now the angel invites us to hear and preach that same transforming word.

Notes

Introduction

1. Theodore Tappert, trans. and ed., *The Book of Concord* (Philadelphia: Fortress Press, 1959), p. 346.

2. Walter Brueggemann, *Cadences of Home: Preaching among Exiles* (Louisville: Westminster/John Knox Press, 1997), p. 29.

3. Anna Quindlen, "Social Conscience," *New York Times*, 4 April 1991, A23.

4. Brueggemann, *Cadences of Home*, p. 36.

5. Mary Oliver, *New and Selected Poems* (Boston: Beacon Press, 1992), p. 98.

6. Larry Rasmussen, *Moral Fragments and Moral Community* (Minneapolis: Fortress Press, 1993), p. 31.

7. Fred Pratt Green, "The Church of Christ in Every Age" (Carol Stream, Ill.: Hope Publishing Co., 1971).

8. Marcus Borg and N. T. Wright, *The Meaning of Jesus: Two Visions* (San Francisco: HarperCollins, 1998), p. 122.

9. Luke Timothy Johnson, *Living Jesus: Learning the Heart of the Gospel* (San Francisco: Harper Collins, 1998), pp. 12, 13.

10. Delores S. Williams, "Reimagining Truth: Traversing the Feminist Christian Backlash," *The Other Side* 30, no. 3 (May-June 1994): 53.

Chapter 1. Grounded in Grace

1. Anne E. Carr, *Transforming Grace: Christian Tradition and Women's Experience* (San Francisco: Harper & Row, 1988), p. 186.

2. Frank A. Thomas, *They Like to Never Quit Praisin' God: The Role of Celebration in Preaching* (Cleveland: United Church Press, 1997), p. 3.

3. Ronald Allen, *The Teaching Sermon* (Nashville: Abingdon Press, 1995), p. 108.

4. Joseph Sittler, *Gravity & Grace: Reflections and Provocations* (Minneapolis: Augsburg, 1986), p. 14.

5. Anne Lamott, *Traveling Mercies: Some Thoughts on Faith* (New York: Anchor Books, 1999), p. 43.

6. Mary Oliver, *A Poetry Handbook* (New York: Harcourt Brace & Company, 1994), p. 122.

7. Gerhard E. Frost, *Seasons of a Lifetime: A Treasury of Meditations* (Minneapolis: Augsburg Press, 1989), p. 41.

8. Paul Tillich, *Shaking of the Foundations* (New York: Charles Scribner's Sons, 1948), pp. 161-62.

9. Ibid., pp. 162, 163.

10. Jane Wagner, *The Search for Signs of Intelligent Life in the Universe* (New York: Harper & Row, 1986), p. 95.

11. Ibid., pp. 95, 98.

12. Ibid., p. 99.

13. Ibid., p. 102.

Chapter 2. Children from Stones: Shaping New Communities

1. Anne Lamott, *Traveling Mercies: Some Thoughts on Faith* (New York: Anchor Books, 1999), p. 143.

2. Jim Wallis, *The Call to Conversion: Recovering the Gospel for These Times* (San Francisco: Harper & Row, 1981), p. 108.

3. Ibid., p. 115.

4. Walter Brueggemann, *Genesis: Interpretation Series* (Atlanta: John Knox Press, 1982), p. 183.

5. Thomas Hoyt, Jr. in Cain Hope Felder, ed., *Stony the Road We Trod: African American Biblical Interpretation* (Minneapolis: Fortress Press, 1991), p. 33.

6. James Forbes, Jr., paraphrase from a videotaped sermon.

7. Janet R. Walton, *Feminist Liturgy: A Matter of Justice* (Collegeville, Minn.: Liturgical Press, 2000), p. 35.

8. Brian Wren, "Bring Many Names" (Carol Stream, Ill.: Hope Publishing Co., 1989).

9. Walter Brueggemann, *Cadences of Home: Preaching among Exiles* (Louisville: Westminster/John Knox Press, 1997), p. 36.

10. Gerhard Frost, *Seasons of a Lifetime: A Treasury of Meditations* (Minneapolis: Augsburg Press, 1989), p. 132.

11. Ibid., p. 57.

12. Ibid., p. 85.

Chapter 3. Testing What Is Written in Stone

1. Rosemary Radford Ruether, *Women-Church: Theology and Practice* (San Francisco: Harper & Row, 1985), p. 34.

2. Ibid., p. 34.

3. Walter Wink uses the term "Jesus' Third Way" between "fight and flight" in *Engaging the Powers: Discernment and Resistance in a World of Domination* (Minneapolis: Fortress Press, 1992), pp. 175-93.

4. James Weldon Johnson, "Lift Every Voice and Sing" in *The United Methodist Hymnal* (Nashville: United Methodist Publishing House, 1989), no. 519.

5. Delores S. Williams, unpublished lecture, "Re-Imagining Revival Conference," St. Paul, Minnesota, April 1998.

6. Walter Wink, "Homosexuality and the Bible" in *Homosexuality and Christian Faith: Questions of Conscience for the Churches*, ed. Walter Wink (Minneapolis: Fortress Press, 1999), p. 47.

7. Janet R. Walton, *Feminist Liturgy: A Matter of Justice* (Collegeville, Minn.: Liturgical Press, 2000), p. 92.

8. Joy M. K. Bussert, *Battered Women: From a Theology of Suffering to an Ethic of Empowerment* (New York: Division for Mission in North America, Lutheran Church in America, 1986). Pastor Bussert cites several stories from interviews with battered women. "For example, one woman in a shelter told me that when she first went to her mother for help, she was told that the abuse was her cross to bear... 'When I couldn't handle it anymore,' she said, 'I could only conclude that it must be my fault and my problem.' When she went to her pastor, he not only signed her up for 'submission classes'—which he taught—but suggested that she view the violence as a test of her capacity for real Christian servanthood" (64).

9. Phyllis Trible, *Texts of Terror: Literary-Feminist Readings of Biblical Narratives* (Philadelphia: Fortress Press, 1984), p. 86. At the end of her chapter on the abused and dismembered concubine, Trible writes: "'Direct your heart to her, take counsel, and speak.' From their

ancient setting, these imperatives move into the present, challenging us to answer anew.... When we direct our hearts to her, what counsel can we take? What word can we speak?" (86).

10. Christopher Morse, *Not Every Spirit: A Dogmatics of Christian Disbelief* (Valley Forge, Penn.: Trinity Press International, 1994), p. 45. This book is a very helpful resource for testing traditional and contemporary teachings. Each chapter ends with "Proposed Disbeliefs" that Christian faith "refuses to believe" about the Word of God, Jesus Christ, the Holy Spirit, creation, humanity, etc.

11. Joseph Sittler, *Gravity & Grace: Reflections and Provocations* (Minneapolis: Augsburg, 1986), pp. 64-65.

12. Elizabeth A. Johnson, *She Who Is: The Mystery of God in Feminist Theological Discourse* (New York: Crossroad, 1992), pp. 13-14.

13. Arland Hultgren, "The Bible in a Reforming Church: Some Gifts and Tasks," in Charles Lutz, ed., *A Reforming Church... Gift and Task: Essays from a Free Conference* (Minneapolis: Kirk House, 1995), p. 43.

14. Sittler, *Gravity & Grace*, p. 65.

15. Hultgren, "The Bible in a Reforming Church," p. 43.

16. Johnson, *She Who Is*, p. 12.

17. "Holy Baptism" in *Lutheran Book of Worship* (Minneapolis: Augsburg Publishing House and Philadelphia: Board of Publication, Lutheran Church in America, 1978), p. 124.

18. Ibid.

Chapter 4. Bearing the Hard Words

1. Douglas Marlette, *There's No Business Like Soul Business* (Atlanta: Peachtree, 1987).

2. Larry Rasmussen, "Jesus and Power," unpublished lecture, p. 3. Rasmussen is paraphrasing a statement by Rabbi Irving Greenberg: "Hope is a dream committed to the discipline of becoming a fact." (From a public forum of The Rainbow Coalition, Jewish-Christian Dialog group, autumn, 1986.)

3. Ibid.

4. Quoted by John Thomas in "A Mystical and Moral Presence: Unity and Renewal in the 21st Century," Address to the Mercersburg Society, June 10, 1998, p. 14.

5. Lenora Tubbs Tisdale, *Preaching as Local Theology and Folk Art* (Minneapolis: Fortress Press, 1997), p. 42.

6. Rasmussen, "Jesus and Power," p. 7.

7. Heidi Neumark, unpublished Bible study, ELCA Consultation on Women and Children Living in Poverty, Chicago, June 26, 1998.

8. Dorothy Bass, ed., *Practicing Our Faith: A Way of Life for Searching People* (San Francisco: Jossey-Bass, 1997), pp. 5, 8, 9.

9. John P. Kretzmann and John L. McKnight, *Building Communities from the Inside Out: A Path Toward Finding and Mobilizing a Community's Assets* (Evanston, Ill.: Center for Urban Affairs and Policy Research, 1993), pp. 150-51. This book contains hundreds of brief vignettes of "provocative alternatives" along with addresses and phone numbers for congregations, agencies, and organizations for those who want in-depth information.

10. Kathleen Norris, *Dakota: A Spiritual Geography* (New York: Ticknor & Fields, 1993), p. 120.

11. W. H. Auden, "Twelve Songs: No. XII" in Edward Mendelson, ed., *W. H. Auden: Collected Poems* (New York: Vintage International, 1991), p. 145.

Chapter 5. Splashing, Bursting Against the Stone

1. Meg Christian, "The Rock Will Wear Away" from the album *Face the Music* (Oakland, Calif.: Olivia Records, 1977).

2. Beverly Harrison, unpublished lecture.

3. Tex Sample, *U.S. Lifestyles and Mainline Churches* (Louisville: Westminster/John Knox Press, 1990), p. 74.

4. Ibid., pp. 74-75.

5. Ibid., pp. 75-76.

6. Books in the area of congregational studies include *Constructing Local Theologies* by Robert J. Schreiter; *Varieties of Religious Presence* by David A. Roozen, William McKinney, and Jackson Carroll; *American Mainline Religion: Its Changing Shape and Future* by Wade Clark Roof and William McKinney; *Preaching as Local Theology and Folk Art* by Leonora Tubbs Tisdale; and many books published by Hartford Seminary and the Alban Institute, Washington, D.C.

7. For detailed information about country music and the church see Tex Sample, *White Soul: Country Music, the Church, and Working Americans* (Nashville: Abingdon Press, 1996).

8. Roxanna Robinson, "If You Invent the Story, You're the First to See How It Ends," *New York Times*, 17 July 2000, E2.

9. "The Common Service: Morning" in *The Hymnal and Order of Service* (Rock Island, Ill.: Augustana Book Concern, 1944), pp. 669-70.

This confession continued in the *Service Book and Hymnal of the Lutheran Church in America,* which was published in 1958 (see pp. 1, 16, and 42).

10. Ellen F. Davis, *Proverbs, Ecclesiastes, and the Song of Songs* (Louisville: Westminster/John Knox Press, 2000), p. 236.

11. Phyllis Trible, *God and the Rhetoric of Sexuality* (Philadelphia: Fortress Press, 1978), p. 161.

12. Krister Stendahl, "Memorandum on Our Bible and Our Sexuality" (Letter to the Evangelical Lutheran Church in America: February 28, 1994), p. 3.

13. Walter Wink, ed., *Homosexuality and Christian Faith: Questions of Conscience for the Churches* (Minneapolis: Fortress Press, 1999). This book of essays, especially Part Two: Biblical Witness, is a very helpful resource for congregational study.

14. Martin Buber, *I and Thou* (New York: Charles Scribner's Sons, 1970), p. 69.

15. Sam Keen, *To a Dancing God* (New York: Harper & Row, 1970), p. 122.

16. Ibid., p. 121.

17. For example, Gunther Bornkamm, "The Authority to 'Bind' and 'Loose' in the Church" in *The Interpretation of Matthew,* ed. Graham Stanton (Philadelphia: Fortress Press, 1983), p. 93.

18. Daniel Patte, *The Gospel According to Matthew* (Philadelphia: Fortress Press, 1987), p. 233.

19. I am indebted to biblical scholar Linda Schearing, associate professor of religious studies at Gonzaga University, for this material on the anesthesia debates, found in unpublished research on the history of the interpretation of Genesis 3.

20. Recent scholarship indicates that the Hebrew word translated "pain" is more accurately translated as "toil" ("I shall increase your toil in childbearing").

21. The texts read at the beginning of the worship service were: Leviticus 13:45-46, Ephesians 5:22-23*a*, Exodus 21:22-25, Mark 10:10-12, Leviticus 15:19, Romans 13:1, Ephesians 6:5, and 1 Timothy 2:11-12. These texts were purposely selected from both First and Second Testaments to avoid any sense that the "Old" is oppressive while the "New" is liberating.

22. Audre Lorde, *A Burst of Light* (Ithaca, New York: Firebrand Books, 1988), p. 120.

Conclusion. Living Stones

1. Walter Brueggemann, *Texts That Linger, Words That Explode: Listening to Prophetic Voices* (Minneapolis: Fortress Press, 2000), p. 1.

2. Ibid.

3. "Holy Communion: Settings One, Two, and Three" in *Lutheran Book of Worship* (Minneapolis: Augsburg Publishing House and Philadelphia: Board of Publication, Lutheran Church in America, 1978), pp. 58, 79, 100.

4. Wild Goose Worship Group, *A Wee Worship Book: Fourth incarnation* (Chicago: GIA Publications, 1999), p. 89.

5. Mary Oliver, *A Poetry Handbook* (New York: Harcourt Brace & Company, 1994), p. 122.